MAMMALS
of the
PACIFIC NORTHWEST
A Pictorial Introduction

*Hope you enjoy
my book,
Jim Christensen*

Photographing chipmunks; a pleasant way to study them, as well as the other mammals of the Pacific Northwest (E.J.L.)

MAMMALS
of the
PACIFIC NORTHWEST
A Pictorial Introduction

by
James R. Christensen
and
Earl J. Larrison

A NORTHWEST NATURALIST BOOK
The University Press of Idaho
A Division of
The Idaho Research Foundation, Inc.
1982

ISBN 0-89301-085-5
Library of Congress Catalog number 82-60054
Copyright © 1982 by the University Press of Idaho
All rights reserved
Manufactured in the United States of America
Printed by the
News-Review Publishing Co., Inc., Moscow, Idaho
Published by the University Press of Idaho
A Division of the Idaho Research Foundation, Inc.
Box 3368, University Station, Moscow, Idaho 83843

CONTENTS

Black-tailed Jackrabbits, illustrating the typical long ears of the "jacks" (J.W.T.)

Common Deer Mouse (12 miles east of Ellensburg, Washington; J.R.C.)

Mountain Beaver (J.W.T.)

Muskrat gathering nesting materials (Pend Oreille Co., Washington; E.J.L.)

Mammals exhibit a considerable diversity of shapes, sizes, and habitats, as these photographs portray.

Desert Bighorn (Cleman Mountain, Yakima Co., Washington; J.R.C.)

INTRODUCTION

Though not as well known as the birds of the Pacific Northwest, the mammals of that region rightly merit our attention for several reasons. First, they represent the most highly evolved group of animals, including, for that matter, man himself. Second, the varied problems of existence have been solved satisfactorily by them in ways that are of interest and value to ourselves as distant cousins. Third, being mostly nocturnal, there is an air of mystery about them, a phantasmagoria of living forms that exist all about us, yet are mostly unknown to us. Finally, some, like the begging squirrels of the national park campgrounds or the trophies of the hunters, are more or less familiar to a number of people, while the vast majority of the mice, for example, are only names and pictures in a book. Unfortunately, a few mammals may get in the way of human progress and need to be known and studied so that we, in our ultimate wisdom, may decide whether or not they are to remain a part of the "wild kingdom".

Mammals, as such, are easily recognizable. The young are born alive and nursed on milk produced by the female for an early period of their lives. The habits of mammals are the most sophisticated of those of all animals and indicate the presence of the highest degree of intelligence and adaptiveness possessed by any part of the animal kingdom. However, more obvious than any of these traits, is the possession of hair which more or less entirely covers the bodies of most mammalian species and is found nowhere else among animals.

It is the purpose of this book to introduce the mammal fauna of the Pacific Northwest to those human citizens of the region who, young or old, layman or professional, may not have had a previous acquaintanceship with these interesting animals. We do this in the book with a variety of pictorial illustrations, including a large number of pen and ink drawings of representative species of each group as well as an assortment of photographs delineating many of the mammals in life as well as a number of scenes of the environments in which they exist.

The text in this pictorial introduction to the mammals of the Pacific Northwest is restricted to brief descriptive accounts of the various species with a short summary of their geographic ranges in the region preceded by a general account giving some of the most important characters of the group or certain representatives of it. Many of these accounts introducing a species group have been selected from previous books on the mammals of the Northwest and thus constitute an anthology of writings from the time of Lewis and Clark to the present. The junior author has been guilty of writing many books on the higher vertebrates of the region, in whole or in part, so must be excused for having included some passages from those books!

The region here treated as the "Pacific Northwest" includes the states of Washington, Oregon, and Idaho and the Canadian province of British Columbia. The distributional ranges given in the species accounts in this book apply only to the animals' occurrence in the Northwest. Many of the forms mentioned occur elsewhere in North America as well.

As had been detailed elsewhere and in the authors' other books, the Pacific Northwest is a region of great physiographic and climatic variety, ranging from the sub-arctic to the Great Basin deserts and from the Pacific Ocean to the Rocky Mountains. Elevations stretch from the mild conditions at sea level to the near polar climates of the highest snow-capped volcanos. Some mammal species live in comparatively comfortable habitats, while others spend their lives in regions of extreme ecological stress. Practically every environmental type in the Northwest contains a large or small assortment of endemic mammals. In all, approximately 169 species make up the region's mammalian fauna. We say "approximately", because mammalogists are not yet in perfect agreement as to the specific identity of certain forms. In this respect, the authors have used, somewhat conservatively, their own judgement, as for example whether there are three or two species of red-backed mice in the region. Most readers of this book will not care. If they can come, by using this work, to recognize a red-backed mouse when they find one, our efforts will not have been in vain.

February, 1982   James R. Christensen
Earl J. Larrison

NOTES

In the species' descriptions that follow, the measurements are for total length and tail length given first in inches and then (in parentheses) in millimeters.

Initials for photo credits are as follows:
E.J.L. · Earl J. Larrison
J.R.C. · James R. Christensen
J.W.T. · J.W. Thompson

Quotations in the following general accounts are from the following:

Bailey, Vernon 1936 THE MAMMALS AND LIFE ZONES OF OREGON Bureau of Biological Survey, U.S. Dept. of Agriculture, Washington, D.C.

Baillie-Grohman, W.A. 1900 FIFTEEN YEARS' OF SPORT AND LIFE IN THE HUNTING GROUNDS OF WESTERN AMERICA AND BRITISH COLUMBIA Horace Cox, London

Hornaday, William T. 1907 CAMP-FIRES IN THE CANADIAN ROCKIES T. Werner Laurie, London

Larrison, Earl J. 1943 "Feral coypus in the Pacific Northwest" MURRELET 24 [1]:3-9

Larrison, Earl J. 1970 WASHINGTON MAMMALS: THEIR HABITS, IDENTIFICATION AND DISTRIBUTION Seattle Audubon Society, Seattle, Washington

Larrison, Earl J. 1976 MAMMALS OF THE NORTHWEST Seattle Audubon Society, Seattle, Washington

Lewis, Meriwether and William Clark HISTORY OF THE EXPEDITION UNDER THE COMMAND OF LEWIS AND CLARK, etc. edited by Elliott Coues Francis P. Harper, New York 1893 (Dover reprint, 1965)

Seton, Ernest T. 1928 THE LIVES OF GAME ANIMALS Charles T. Brandford, Boston

Sheldon, Charles 1930 THE WILDERNESS OF DENALI Scribners, New York

Taylor, Walter P. and William T. Shaw 1927 MAMMALS AND BIRDS OF MOUNT RAINIER NATIONAL PARK U.S. Govt. Printing Office, Washington, D.C.

MAMMALS OF THE PACIFIC NORTHWEST

A Summary

As arranged in this book, the mammals of the Pacific Northwest occur in some 37 groups, including the seals but excluding the whales. This variety of mammalian forms reflects the diversity of environmental types to be found in the region. Such a broad spectrum of species groups makes for a fascinating study of this vertebrate class in our part of North America.

A few Northwest species are not native, having been voluntarily or involuntarily introduced by man. Examples are the American Opossum and the Old World rats and mice, besides a few others.

Of the native forms, we have a generous supply of shrews, reflecting not only the presence of moist mild climates but a boreal element in the region. Four species of moles make up that interesting group. Mirroring their immense order, some 18 species of bats have been found in the Northwest, a considerable variety but animals that are little known and seldom identified. Rabbits, hares, and pikas are few with us, but some species are widely distributed and the more diurnal forms occasionally seen. A veritable living fossil is the Mountain Beaver of the humid coastal areas. Among the best known of the mammals, due largely to their diurnal habits, are numerous chipmunks, marmots, ground squirrels, and tree squirrels. Very few areas in the Northwest are without a chipmunk. The rocky places have their marmots and the drier interior regions are supplied during the summer months with an abundance of ground squirrels. The forests and woodlands contain populations of tree squirrels, as also the nocturnal and seldom-seen flying squirrels.

Open habitats are provided with pocket gophers, while the deserts and semi-deserts contain some six species of pocket mice, kangaroo mice, and kangaroo rats. Many streams and lakes contain beavers with their interesting dams and lodges and occasional appearances in the twilight hours. Probably most numerous of the mice are the long-tailed harvest and deer mice, one species of which, the Common Deer Mouse, is the most abundant in the region. Related to this assemblage is the short-tailed, but rather irregularly distributed Northern Grasshopper Mouse. Relatives also are three species of wood rats of thievery fame.

The stocky-bodied short-tailed voles are abundant in many habitats and few parts of the Pacific Northwest are without at least one kind. They are mostly to be found in meadow and grassland areas, marshes, bogs, and similar non-wooded types. Perhaps even more widespread than the beaver along waterways and aquatic shores is the mild-mannered muskrat. Moist grassy and brushy places near water are homes for the seldom-seen but attractive little jumping mice. Most of our readers have seen a porcupine, never abundant, but widely distributed in the Northwest.

Who of our readers has not heard the call of the coyote? Most numerous in the open areas of the interior, it nevertheless inhabits almost the entire region in spite of an almost continual warfare that man has unfortunately waged against it. Less commonly encountered are four other species of the dog tribe. Two kinds of bears are in our region and probably are most commonly to be seen in the great national parks. Other carnivorous species include the raccoons and the some dozen members of the weasel gang, as well as the three species of cats that occur in the Northwest. Since they occasionally are seen along salt water beaches or close inshore, we have included the several forms of seals and sea lions that visit or live in our territory.

Only 10 species of hoofed mammals variously occur in the Northwest, but are of great value to us as many are seen and enjoyed by campers and hikers and several are of considerable value as being among the leading game and trophy species of North America.

This, then, is a rapid survey of the mammal fauna of the Pacific Northwest. Some species you may never see, but others you may come to know and enjoy intimately. Let us now take you on a more extended visit with them in this book!

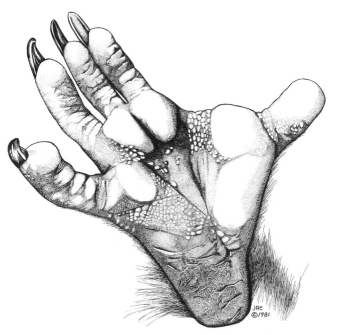

Underside of the Opossum hind foot

Mother Opossum with her family

OPOSSUMS

The American, or Virginia, Opossum is an animal unique in several ways. First, it is not native to the Pacific Northwest, having spread from California or perhaps having been introduced into our region. Here, its success has been various, thriving in the mild-weathered coastal areas, but not penetrating the more contrastively-seasoned interior. Second, the species is one of those forms that biologists frequently refer to as "living fossils" which have graced this planet with little or no structural change for millions of years — eons that have seen the rise and fall of many other species. The Opossum is a marsupial, one of the almost — but not quite — modern mammals. Primitive in structure and reproduction, it is unique among North American mammal types.

Not particularly esteemed for either its food value or fur in our Northwest region, the Opossum is strictly a novelty. If anything, it may be a nuisance under certain circumstances when unprotected henhouses or other potential food supplies are conveniently available.

As an example of how exotic species such as this one may enter and prosper in an area, the following paragraphs are quoted from THE MAMMALS AND LIFE ZONES OF OREGON by Vernon Bailey published in 1936. Incidently, this is the first of a series of quotations scattered through this book which are derived from classical, as well as recent, mammalian literature. We hope that readers will find these passages of nostalgic, as well as informative, value:

Jewett and Dobyns (1929, p. 351) have provided an interesting account of the Virginia opossum in Oregon. During the past 6 or 7 years, they reported fur trappers along McKay and Birch Creeks and tributaries in Umatilla County had taken opossums in traps set for mink and skunk. There is knowledge of 50 or more being taken in this section. During the trapping season of 1927 and 1928 at least 12 were taken by local trappers. Besides those taken along these streams signs of them have been noted along the Umatilla River above Pendleton, and there are unverified reports of them along the Walla Walla River above Milton. They seem to be well established and thriving in this part of the State.

One collected on September 9, 1982, in Umatilla County and sent to the Biological Survey for identification proved to be typical *Didelphis virginiana virginiana*. Investigations brought to light records of at least four opossums brought into Umatilla County and liberated between 1910 and 1921. Sam Walker, an old pioneer on McKay Creek, told of a pair of opossums being liberated by one of his neighbors about 1912, and Walker had one that escaped about the same time.

L.E. Roy, of Pilot Rock, reported that one sent to him from Oklahoma had escaped about 1921. For such rapid breeders here was ample material for stocking a new region where food and climate are so favorable to the natural requirements of the species. Fortunately the opossums have sufficient value for food, fur, and sport to preclude any danger of their becoming a pest.

Bailey: MAMMALS AND LIFE ZONES OF OREGON

NORTHWEST SPECIES

AMERICAN OPOSSUM *Didelphis virginiana* 30-12 (750-300)

Size of a domestic cat, but with a long pointed snout, long naked tail, and grayish body with a white face. Black ears and feet. Occurs in bottomland in woods and along streams, as well as farmlands and scattered acreage plots. Introduced or has spread into the lower elevations west of the Cascades and along the Columbia and Snake Rivers to southeastern Washington and adjacent Idaho. Most numerous in the Puget Sound area.

Water Shrew

SHREWS

Shrews [order Insectivora] are the smallest of mammals. They are furred with thick soft coats, except for their tails which are nearly hairless. Their snouts are sharply pointed, their eyes small, and their legs, though short, can carry them about rapidly. Shrews have a row of small sharp teeth extending from the incisors continuously to the molars with no intervening space or diastema, such as is found in rodents. Being so small, they have a very high metabolic rate, burning up "fuel" rapidly. Accordingly, they must be almost constantly in search of food. Shrews are mostly insectivorous, but consume almost any animal life they can subdue, even small mice. Tiny and secretive, shrews are seldom seen, though they are widespread and at least one species occurs in every natural or quasi-natural habitat....

The rushing waters of Goat Creek in the Cascades near Mount Rainier National Park coursed down through the dense hemlock forest, plunging here over a tiny waterfall, slowing there to create a dark pool. The banks of the stream were moss-covered with scattered patches of bunchberry and in more shaded places a stalk or two of Indian pipe. The great trees overhead screened out most of the sun, creating a day-time scene of semi-twilight between intervals of darkest night. A few birds, mostly kinglets and varied thrushes, sang in the dense canopy above. Most of the sound came from the tumbling waters of the creek.

In this idyllic place, a fifteen-year old boy lay motionless on his stomach on a little shelf above the flashing waters, his attention concentrated on a tiny, grayish, fish-like form that dived and swam through the moving water. At times, the animal would come to the surface and swim easily and rapidly; then, it would dive to the bottom, seemingly foraging over the gravel. The layer of air surrounding the diver made it look at times like a large, elongated, grayish bubble. Here was certainly a first-class mystery which was not solved till the little animal at last came to shore on a tiny mossy beach just above a miniature waterfall. It stopped for a moment to shake itself and the black upperparts and grayish underparts revealed the mite to be a Water Shrew. The boy had been spellbound by this episode and determined to learn more of the ways of nature's furry citizens. Thus was born an interest in mammals that the author [Larrison] has carried with him ever since that long-ago afternoon spent by Goat Creek.

Many kinds of mammals are characterized by three kinds of species: those that are common and widespread in distribution, those of average numbers and medium-sized ranges, and those that are rare in their small restricted zones of occurrence. The Preble's Shrew is definitely one of the last group. A small shrew, light brownish above and silvery gray below, it seems to prefer small isolated marshes in the dry country particularly in yellow pine or lodgepole pine forests.

Very little is known about the habitat of this rare mammal. Here would be an interesting species life history monograph project. Perhaps, like other (Northwest) mammals, it is not so rare, when one finds out exactly its biotype. So much is yet to be learned of the natural history of our mammals and so few students are willing to put in the long hours of field work under conditions of blazing sun and whirling snow to fill in the many gaps in our knowledge of these matters. What is needed, particularly in [the Northwest] is a re-birth of the old-time interest in field research held by such Washington and Pacific Northwest naturalists of a bygone time as John Edson, D.E. Brown, Clark Streator, Stanley Jewett, Leo Couch, George Cantwell, William T. Shaw, Theo Scheffer, Storrs H. Lyman, E.B. Webster, and many others.

Preble's Shrew was named by Hartley H.T. Jackson, the great authority on North American shrews, for Edward Alexander Preble, who collected the first specimen at Jordan Valley, Oregon in 1915. Preble became well known as a field biologist for the old Biological Survey, working in many parts of the West and Far North.

[The Vagrant Shrew] is probably the most widely distributed and abundant shrew in [the Pacific Northwest]. It occurs in a variety of

Vagrant Shrew (Kendrick, Idaho; J.R.C.)

habitats, both wet and dry, and is the shrew most likely to be found in dry meadows and fields. It is, however, rather strongly restricted to the low and intermediate elevations....Like most shrews, considerable care must be used on its identification.

Rotten logs, rock piles, dead grass mats, and other forms of cover will often yield specimens of these animals. They have frequently been caught in traps set in meadow mouse runways. They may burrow to a small degree in the soft soil of the forest floor, but more often travel beneath the blanket of leaves. [Larrison] has captured a number in places where they were common by standing motionless in the woods and listening for the scratching in the leaf mat as they made their way through the dry brittle cover. When one came within reach a sudden grab would secure the specimen. A few times, he merely dropped his hat on an individual scurrying along the surface. The shock of this sudden occurrence was usually enough to kill the shrew.

Vagrant Shrews are active at all hours, though busiest in the early evening. Dormancy during the winter is not entered, as the pushed-up ridge on a snow surface where a shrew has been "snow-swimming" is not an unusual sight in the winter forest. Temporarily reduced metabolic rates enable shrews to pass inactive hours without untoward oxidation of food in the body. Vagrant Shrews molt from the winter to the summer pelage in the spring and acquire the winter coat in October....

Unlike the Water Shrew, [the Marsh Shrew] ap-

pears to prefer marshes, bogs, areas along standing water, and slow-moving streams. As Vernon Bailey mentioned in his classic book on the mammals of Oregon, these are more mud shrews than water shrews. They seem to represent a half-way development between the strongly aquatic *palustris* and the more terrestrial soricines....

[Larrison] first became acquainted with the species in making studies of the small mammals of the Chase Lake area, now in the northern suburbs of Seattle. Chase Lake is, or was, a typical sphagnum bog complex, formerly so common in glaciated areas of the Puget Sound basin.

Larrison: WASHINGTON MAMMALS

* * *

The twelve species of shrews that occur in the Pacific Northwest all belong to the genus *Sorex*. While thus ostensibly closely related, they nevertheless exhibit unique features, each of them, as regards characters and ecological and geographic distribution. We present here a summary of how a group of mammals have sorted themselves out ecologically and geographically in a region. The Cinereous, or Ashy or Masked Shrew as it is sometimes called, is primarily a denizen of the deep dark forests and woods, frequenting particularly the drier parts of such habitats. In the northernmost parts of North America, however, it is to be found in tundra situations. This divergence of environmental

Track of a snow-swimming shrew (Pend Oreille Co., Washington; E.J.L.)

12

Arctic-Alpine habitat of the Dusky Shrew (Mt. Pilchuck, Washington; E.J.L.)

Habitat of the Dusky Shrew (Granite Cr., Washington; E.J.L.)

preference is perhaps to be expected in a mammalian species having such a wide transcontinental distribution. The diminutive Preble's Shrew, as previously related, has a much more restricted range, being found so far in Oregon, Washington, Idaho, and Montana, as regards the region here covered. Its chosen haunts are those of streamside and boggy springs, as well as riparian brush, grass, and forbs. *Sorex vagrans,* the Vagrant, or Wandering, Shrew has a more southern distribution and while showing some variation in ecologic preference is with us more an animal of the grasslands, grain fields, and open brush, where it is often the one shrew species most likely to be met. It is primarily a lowland species and seldom reaches high up into the mountains. On the other hand, the Dusky Shrew, a larger and darker form, is a more northern type and is often trapped in muskegs, wet places in the forest, and in the wet subalpine habitats, being a more montane and alpine type.

A larger shrew than the above, the Pacific Shrew, is restricted, as regards the Pacific Northwest, to southwestern Oregon where it has been found in moist, marshy, brushy places in the coastal strip. It seems to be particularly fond of decayed and rotten fallen logs. The Ashland Shrew, with its unique short and triangular rostrum in the skull, a technical feature, has a very limited range, as far as is known, in the vicinity of Ashland, Oregon. In contrast, the distinctively

marked and much larger Water Shrew, has a wide range in the northern part of the North American temperate zone, dipping down into the Northwest and following the shores and margins of mountain streams and lakes. Its foraging is mainly done in water where it swims and dives with ease. Mouse-sized, black above and whitish below, it is easily identified and may occasionally be seen swimming in whitewater mountain or subalpine streams in daylight. Also showing a strong attachment to the aquatic, the Marsh [or Bendire's] Shrew is primarily a Pacific Northwest species where it occurs in lowland bogs and marshes as well as along woodland ponds. It seldom passes up into the montane and subalpine, except on the northern slopes of the Olympic Mountains in northwestern Washington. Sphagnum bogs in coastal areas are favored habitats and Vernon Bailey in his book on Oregon mammals (1936) refers to them as "mud shrews" rather than "water shrews".

Barely entering the Pacific Northwest fauna by occurring in northeastern British Columbia, the attractive tri-colored Arctic Shrew reflects its preferred tundra habitat of the far North by being found mostly in bogs in its Northwest range. Also distinctively marked, both in coloration and habitat, is the Trowbridge's Shrew with its solid dark gray color, sharply bicolored tail, and predilection for the dense coniferous forest habitat of the lowlands and lower slopes of the

13

mountains in the west of Cascade crest area, for most records.

Unlike the preceding species which show a preference for dense more or less moist environments, the grayish whitish Merriam's Shrew is a denizen of the deserts, being found in sagebrush and grassland areas in the Upper Sonoran Zone. Smallest of these tiny mammals is the Pygmy Shrew which has been found so far only in the Rockies and related areas of the Pacific Northwest and in much of the interior of British Columbia. It would seem to occur in relatively dry wooded areas, although the few specimens taken in the Northwest indicate a certain variety of ecologic preference.

NORTHWEST SPECIES

CINEREOUS SHREW *Sorex cinereus* 4 1/8 · 1 3/4 (105-44)
A medium-sized light grayish-brown shrew that is brighter in color than the other Northwest brown shrews. Technically, the 4th unicuspid tooth on the side of the jaw is smaller than the preceding (3rd) unicuspid. Moist forest areas in foothills and mountains (except Oregon).

PREBLE'S SHREW *Sorex preblei* 3 1/2 · 1 5/16 (90-34)
A small shrew (total length less than 100 mm) with light brownish upper parts and whitish under parts. Springs, bogs, and stream riparian growth, often in pine woods. Eastern and central Oregon, southeastern Washington, extreme western Idaho, and western Montana.

A warm water creek on Mt. Pilchuck, Washington — habitat of the Marsh Shrew (E.J.L.)

VAGRANT SHREW *Sorex vagrans* 4 1/8 · 1 5/8 (104-42)
A medium-sized brownish shrew with a tail less than 50 mm and weakly bicolored. Brownish above and buffy gray below. The 3rd unicuspid is distinctly smaller than the 4th. Very similar to the Dusky Shrew but the median tines between the 1st upper incisors in *S. vagrans* are very small and located at the upper edge of the pigment and set off from the latter by a gap in color. Damp areas in meadows, brush, fern jungles, weedy patches, etc. in lowlands and foothills in the Northwestern states and extreme southern British Columbia.

DUSKY SHREW *Sorex montilcolus* (=*Sorex obscurus*) 4 3/8-1 7/8 (110-47)
Similar to the Vagrant Shrew but slightly larger and darker. Brownish gray below. Moist habitats, mostly in montane and alpine areas.

PACIFIC SHREW *Sorex pacificus* 6 · 2 3/8 (155-60)
A large shrew with dark brown upper parts paling slightly on the under parts. Tail long and not bicolored. Damp marshes and brush in coastal western Oregon.

ASHLAND SHREW *Sorex trigonirostris* 3 7/8 · 1 3/8 (100-35)
A small short-tailed shrew, grayish brown above and pale grayish below. Occurs along streams in the Ashford area of western Oregon in the Northwest.

WATER SHREW *Sorex palustris* 6 1/8 · 3 (156-76)
A large shrew with blackish or dark gray upper parts and whitish under parts and a sharply bicolored tail. The large feet have the toes fringed with long hairs. White water streams and montane and alpine lake shores of the mountains, more or less throughout the Northwest.

Sagebrush habitat of the Merriam's Shrew (Cassia Co., Idaho; E.J.L.)

14

MARSH SHREW *Sorex bendirei* 6-3 (150-76)
A large shrew, blackish above and grayish black or brownish below. The Olympic Mountains form is lighter, brownish above and light brown to buffy below. The tail is of one color or very weakly bicolored. Marshes and sphagnum bogs of the lowlands of southwestern British Columbia, western Washington, and western Oregon.

ARCTIC SHREW *Sorex articus* 4 1/2 - 1 5/8 (115-42)
A medium-sized tricolored shrew with dark brownish to blackish back, brownish sides, and grayish to grayish-brown under parts. In riparian growth near water in northeastern British Columbia.

TROWBRIDGE'S SHREW *Sorex trowbridgei* 5 - 2 1/3 (125-58)
A medium-sized blackish or sooty-gray shrew only slightly lighter on the under parts and with a conspicuous bicolored tail [black above, white below]. Dense coniferous forests in southwestern British Columbia, western Washington, and western Oregon.

MERRIAM'S SHREW *Sorex merriami* 3 2/3 - 1 2/5 (90-36)
A small shrew with light grayish upper parts and whitish under parts. Tail strongly bicolored (brown above and white below). Sagebrush, sage grass, or grasslands in the arid desert areas of eastern Washington, eastern Oregon, and southern Idaho.

PYGMY SHREW *Sorex hoyi* 3 2/5 - 1 1/8 (85-28)
A very small shrew, the smallest mammal in North America. Upper parts reddish brown, sides tannish, and under parts white. Tail bicolored and very short. Technically, only 3 unicuspid teeth are visible on the side of the upper jaw, when the upper lip is pushed back. Dry coniferous woods of eastern and central British Columbia, northeastern Washington, northern Idaho, and northwestern Montana.

Montane coniferous forest habitat of the Trowbridge's Shrew (Mt. Pilchuck, Washington; E.J.L.)

Coast Mole (anterior view)

MOLES

These beautiful big furry moles [Townsend's Mole] are abundant in most of the open rich valley country of western Oregon, where their presence is easily recognized by the ridged runways and large black mounds of earth. Occasionally their ridges and mounds are found in the more open woods but always are more abundant and conspicuous in meadows, fields, and lawns. The animals are rarely seen except by some prying naturalist, as they spend most of their lives below the surface of the ground. Unlike the eastern moles, however, their minute eyes can be opened and seem to be functional, and there is some evidence that the moles occasionally come out upon the surface of the ground at night. Occasionally one is seen when a board is suddenly lifted from the ground, or a log rolled over, but most of their active lives they spend underground, extending long tunnels just below the surface in search of insect food, or digging deeper burrows a foot or two below the surface, and from these burrows pushing out the loose earth in the little rough mounds so familiar to all. These mounds vary from 6 inches to 2 feet in diameter, and 4 inches to a foot in height, and are easily distinguished from those of the pocket gopher by the absence of any trace of a closed doorway.

The mole does not appear at the surface even while pushing up the earth but remains safely hidden below, and when through with one mound leaves the terminal part of the burrow closed as it goes on to extend the tunnel and throw out the next mound of refuse at a distance of 2 to 6 feet from the last. Often these mounds extend in an irregular line of 10 or 20 rods across a field, but more generally they wind about and crisscross each other until sometimes the surface of the ground is half covered with the black earth recently brought up from below.

Theo H. Scheffer, who has made a close study of these animals and their habits, says that much of the real life of the moles is lived in the deeper burrows, while the hollow ridges near the surface are mainly feeding runs and passageways, sometimes used but once as the animal pushes by while in search of food. Others are used regularly, not only by the moles but by many small rodents that take advantage of this cover to penetrate fields and gardens and feed upon the farmers crops.

BREEDING HABITS. — Scheffer says that Townsend's mole mates in February and that the young are born in the latter part of March, and develop with astonishing rapidity. By the last of May they are scarcely distinguishable from the adults. There are usually 3 in a litter of young, but sometimes only 2, and still more rarely 4. They are found in rudely constructed nests of grass and stubble, leaves, and rootlets in hollowed-out chambers along the runways. Apparently there is but one litter of young a year, as the well-protected life of the mole insures a sufficient abundance of individuals to balance the food supply. Nearly blind as they are, they would never be so short-sighted as to exterminate or reduce too greatly the abundance of the insect life on which they feed.

FOOD HABITS. — Moles are primarily insectivorous. According to Scheffer, Wight, and Moore, they subsist mainly upon earthworms, ground-inhabiting insects and insect larvae, spiders, and centipedes, and occasionally eat a small amount of sprouting grain and seeds, such as corn, peas, wheat, and oats. In captivity they ravenously eat fresh meat, beefsteak, birds, fish, or almost any kind of meat, but soon starve if given only grain and roots (Scheffer, 1922, p. 11; Wight, 1928, p. 31; Moore, 1933, p. 38).

Their activity and strength are astonishing and their appetites almost insatiable. If given food to their liking they will eat more than their own weight each day, and without abundance of food they quickly starve. They drink freely and soon die if deprived of water.

ECONOMIC STATUS. — While the food habits of these moles show them to be almost wholly beneficial to man, they are often the unintentional cause of great annoyance by scattering their mounds of earth over the surface of the

Shrew-mole

18

Mole hills of the Townsend's Mole (Seattle, Washington; E.J.L.)

ground, in fields and meadows and golf links and on well-kept lawns. They also loosen up the surface of the ground with numerous burrows that allow the soil to dry out and in midsummer to kill or injure the grass and growing crops, and also afford cover to rodents that come in to feed upon the crops. Fortunately, however, their beautiful velvety fur has a value sufficient to make their trapping profitable where they are abundant, and thus lead to control of any overabundance of the species.

Bailey: MAMMALS AND LIFE ZONES OF
OREGON

* * *

Unfortunately mole fur has little value for use in garments at present, unlike the situation in the 1930s and earlier years when it was used especially for collars and trimming on men's fine overcoats.

NORTHWEST SPECIES

SHREW-MOLE *Neurotrichus gibbsi* 4 3/5 · 1 3/4 (115-44)
Small mouse-or shrew-sized, sooty or blackish gray in color, with a long mole-like snout and short hairy tail. Fore feet with moderately long claws. Prefers moist forests with dense undergrowth from sea level to the Cascade crest on the west side, occasionally penetrating to the east slopes of the range. Usually in moist places. Mostly in western Washington and Oregon and southwestern British Columbia.

TOWNSEND'S MOLE *Scapanus townsendi* 8 4/5 · 1 2/3 (210-41)
Large mole with velvety fur (sometimes with brownish or purplish luster). Tail naked; snout long and not hairy. The large broad fore feet with long flattened nails distinctive. Moist meadows, lawns, and agricultural fields, mostly in lowlands but also in the subalpine areas of the northern Olympic Mountains. Occurs west of the Cascades in the Pacific Northwest.

COAST MOLE *Scapanus orarius* 6 1/2 · 1 4/5 (165-35)
Very similar to the Townsend's Mole, but smaller. Color

Forest habitat of the Shrew-mole (King Co., Washington; E.-J.L.)

19

varies according to subspecies from sooty black to coppery or silvery. Wooded or brushy areas from lowlands to sub-alpine zones in southwestern British Columbia; western, central, and southeastern Washington; western and northern Oregon; and extreme west-central Idaho.

BROAD-FOOTED MOLE *Scapanus latimanus* 7 - 1 3/8 (180-36)
Grayish to light brownish in color with soft silky fur, very broad fore feet, and relatively hairy tail. Dry open woods in southcentral Oregon.

Coast Mole (Yakima, Washington; J.R.C)

Relative sizes of the Pacific Northwest Moles (left to right, Townsend's, Broad-footed, Coast, and Shrew) (E.J.L.)

BATS

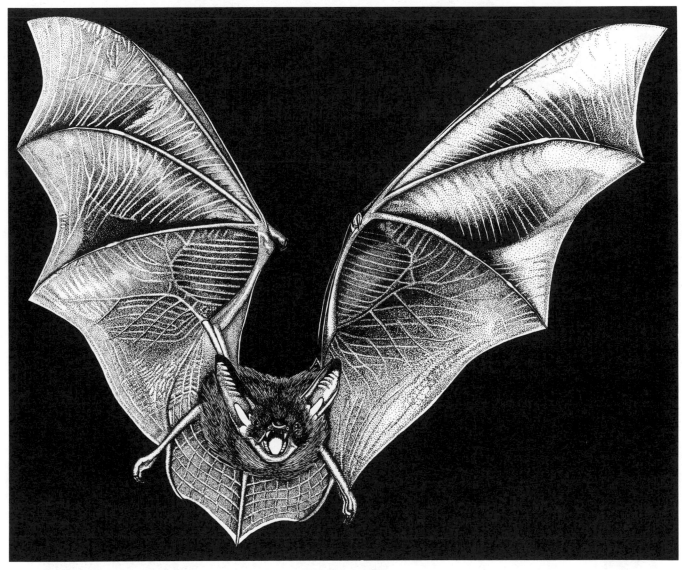

Big Brown Bat

The Order Chiroptera, the bats, is unique in that its members comprise the only group of flying mammals. The toes of bats have become greatly lengthened to form attachments for a nearly naked membrane which extends to the hind legs and then between the latter to enclose the tail. This allows these mammals, unlike other "flying" mammals such as the flying squirrels (which actually glide) to have powers of true sustained flight. Bats' aerial navigation, which allows them to make exceedingly intricate maneuvers both in the laboratory and outside in order to avoid obstacles and to capture food, is accomplished by means similar to sonar. The animals utter short bursts of sound with frequencies between 25,-000 and 75,000 cycles per second and receive echoes as the sounds rebound from objects in their path. Since the human ear can detect sounds of only 20,000 cycles per second at the most, we are unable to hear the bats. Definite squeaks well within the range of human hearing, however, are also given by bats both while they are in flight and at rest. Some of these animals are known to make annual migrations similar to

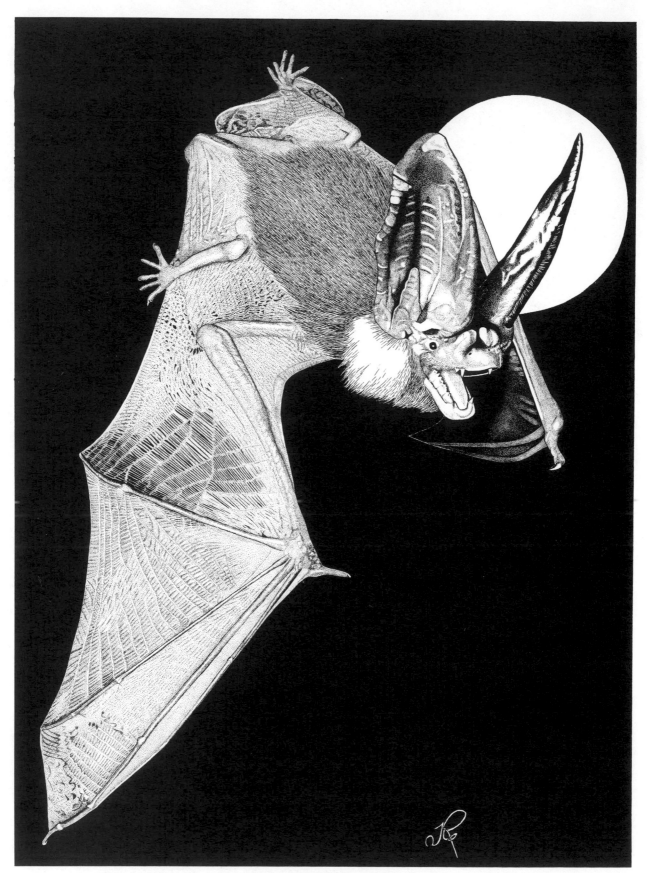

Townsend's Big-eared Bat

those of birds and banding studies have shown them to return to the same cave or tree in the spring. Other species prefer to become torpid and pass the months of food scarcity in suspended animation. All bats found in [the Pacific Northwest] belong to the Family Vespertilionidae, the so-called "evening bats" ....

Bats are for the most part harmless and interesting denizens of the twilight hours, as far as most of us are concerned. They may, however, become a nuisance in attics of homes, particularly the less tightly-built summer cabins. Prevention of bat entry is most important with care taken to stop up all possible places where they might get into the building. In many summer homes (and some in the cities) it has been common practice by the builders to leave an opening above the projecting roof joist where it comes out through the wall. These are excellent places for bats (and other animals) to enter the attic. The author (Larrison) has had good results in keeping bats out by sprinkling several pounds of naphthalene flakes or moth balls (the flakes do the job quicker) on the floor of the attic or space under the roof. This chemical tends to discourage the residence of flying squirrels, pack rats, and tree squirrels, as well.

Larrison: WASHINGTON MAMMALS

Hoary Bat (Naches, Washington; J.R.C.)

The bat is an animal of the twilight. Appearing as the sun dips below the horizon it is best seen against the crimson of the closing day.

On drunken wings the flitting bat
Goes staggering athwart the gloom.

It weaves between the slim candlelike alpine fir tips until, drawing nearer, it swirls through the eddying smoke of the camp fire. As the gloom settles, filling the near-ground spaces and blending the dark foliage with the shades of earth, it descends to a lower level.

The bat is an insect-eating mammal with sharp cuspid teeth well suited for the seizure of its

Little Brown Bat (Kendrick, Idaho, J.R.C.)

23

aerial prey. It is adapted for flight by the development of long bony fingers which are furnished with a membrane of great pliancy, extending from the finger tips to the legs and on to the tail. When at rest the wings are folded along the sides of the body and, remarkable as it may seem, the bat hangs itself up to sleep by the short-toed hind feet, head downward. During the day the bat hides away from the sunlight in dark places about buildings, usually at some distance from the ground. In the mountains it often edges its way under the partly detached bark of some old dead stub or finds shelter in the thick foliage.

Like those of shrews and moles, its eyes are not well developed, and probably its sense of sight is not of much assistance in securing prey, though unquestionably slight differences of light and darkness can be appreciated. The large ears of bats in general suggest that the sense of hearing is highly developed. J. Grinnell has suggested that the bat hunts its insect food by sound, and says: "Even the wing strokes of a tiny miller must be distinctly audible to the bat, which snaps it up so unerringly, and the droning of a June beetle must sound to the bat as penetrating as the roar of an airplane motor does to us".... The sense of touch, too, may function largely in enabling the bat to avoid obstacles which can neither be seen nor heard.

Taylor and Shaw: MAMMALS AND BIRDS
OF MOUNT RAINIER NATIONAL PARK

* * *

To those of us, particularly the young biologists, who find the explanations of most major phenomena of nature to be a *fait accompli,* it is interesting to read of the first glimmerings of knowledge as the suspicion of Joseph Grinnell that sound had something to do with the bat's securing of insect food, a process now well known.

The dozen and a half species of bats in the Pacific Northwest inhabit a variety of environments, though most seem to prefer wooded areas and dry country cliffs and out-croppings. Old buildings, caves, and abandoned mine shafts are also frequented. In short, habitats that offer both an adequate insect food supply and the type of

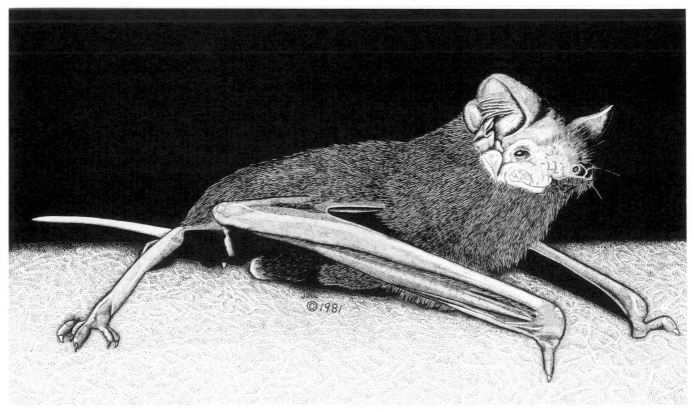

Brazilian Free-tailed Bat

shelter needed for passing the inactive hours in safety. The distribution and habits of our bats in the Northwest region are imperfectly known — but these are not easy mammals to study. Only a lifetime of dedicated devotion to the working out of their ways of life will suffice to increase our knowledge of these unique animals.

For most of us, field identification of bats on the wing is very difficult, if not largely impossible, due to the difficulty of getting an adequate view of their characteristics.

NORTHWEST SPECIES

CALIFORNIA BROWN BAT *Myotis californicus* 3 1/4 · 1 1/2 (82-38)
Small bat with yellowish or reddish brown fur (paler below). Ears dark brown and extending beyond tip of nose when laid forward. Membranes dark brown. Hind feet small, 6 mm or less in length. Wooded areas near water throughout most of the Northwest.

SMALL-FOOTED BROWN BAT *Myotis subulatus* 3 3/16 · 1 1/8 (81-40)
Very similar to the California Brown Bat but with blackish nose and face, slightly larger ears, and tip of tail free of tail membrane. Color of pelage yellowish to golden brown. Open desert type habitats east of the Cascades and in southern Idaho.

YUMA BROWN BAT *Myotis yumanensis* 3 3/8 · 1 3/8 (85-35)
A small bat with buffy or light brownish upper parts and whitish belly. Anterior and posterior parts of the wings are whitish, with the remainder of the wing membranes dark brownish. The interfemoral (tail) membrane is sparsely haired and translucent. The fur of the upper parts is dull. Prefers clearings in forests, both lowland and montane, in southern British Columbia and remainder of the lower Pacific Northwest.

KEEN'S BROWN BAT *Myotis keeni* 3 1/2 · 1 4/5 (88-35)
A small bat with glossy brownish fur and dark brownish or blackish ears and wings. Ears, when laid forward, extend about a quarter of an inch beyond the nose. Clearings and river margins in forested area of western Washington and western British Columbia.

LITTLE BROWN BAT *Myotis lucifugus* 3 2/5 · 1 3/8 (85-39)
Small bat, yellowish brown above (with burnished cast to fur) and pale or light buff below. Wings, tail membranes, feet, and ears are blackish brown. Ears, when laid forward, do not extend past the nose. Often found near water in a variety of habitats, throughout the Northwest.

LONG-LEGGED BROWN BAT *Myotis volans* 3 1/2 · 1 1/2 (90-38)
A small bat, cinnamon brown above and light brown to buf-

Silver-haired Bat (Naches, Washington; J.R.C.)

fy below. Fur is long and soft and extends halfway down the femur and along under side of the wing membrane to the elbow. Ears short, not reaching beyond tip of nose. Forested and broken country in southern British Columbia and the northwest states.

FRINGED BROWN BAT *Myotis thysanodes* 3 1/4 · 1 1/2 (85-37)
Similar to the Long-eared Brown Bat but with shorter ears. Body is uniformly yellow brown to dark olive in color. A conspicuous fringe of short stiff hairs on the free edge of the tail membrane. Southcentral British Columbia, interior Washington, Oregon, western Idaho, southwestern Montana.

LONG-EARED BROWN BAT *Myotis evotis* 3 1/2 · 1 5/8 (88-41)
A small myotis with light to medium brown upper parts, pale brown under parts, and black ears and wing and tail membranes. Ears are long, extending 6-7 mm beyond the tip of the nose when laid forward. The hind (free) edge of the tail membrane with a sparse fringe of hairs. Forested areas thoughout the Northwest, excepting northern British Columbia.

SILVER-HAIRED BAT *Lasionycteris noctivagans* 4 · 1 5/8 (100-40)
A medium-sized bat with dark brown to sooty brown pelage

Pallid Bat

frosted with whitish tips to the hairs (especially on lower half of the back). Basal half of tail membrane furred on upper surface. Clearings and areas along water in forests throughout most of the Northwest.

WESTERN PIPISTREL *Pipistrellus hesperus* 3 · 1 3/16 (75-30)
Very small bat, buffy to light brownish gray in color, with blackish feet, membranes, ears, and face. Desert canyons in southeastern and central Washington, eastern Oregon, and southcentral Idaho.

BIG BROWN BAT *Eptesicus fuscus* 4 1/2 · 1 7/8 (116-48)
A medium-sized to large reddish-brown or brownish bat with blackish wing and tail membranes and ears. Ears short, barely reaching to tip of the nose when laid forward. Habitats near open water in forests as well as settled areas, both rural and suburban throughout most of the Pacific Northwest (except central and northern British Columbia).

RED BAT *Nycteris borealis* 4 2/5 · 2 (110-50)
Medium-sized bat, reddish in color with scattered white-tipped hairs and roundish ears. Upper surface of the tail membrane is fur-covered. Varied habitats. May occur rarely

west of the Cascades from southwestern British Columbia southward.

HOARY BAT *Nycteris cinerea* 5 1/2 · 2 1/4 (140-58)
A large yellowish-gray or light brownish bat with white-tipped hairs giving a "hoary" appearance. Under parts light colored. Upper surface of tail membrane covered with white-tipped hairs. Wings sooty gray with light spots at wrists and elbows. Ears round and margined with black. Frequents clearings in forests and wooded residential areas throughout most of the Northwest (except central and northern British Columbia).

SPOTTED BAT *Euderma maculatum* 4 3/8 · 2 7/16 (110-50)
A medium-sized bat, blackish above (with three prominent white spots) and white below, with very long ears. Apparently very rare in the drier parts of southern Idaho and eastern Oregon.

TOWNSEND'S BIG-EARED BAT *Plecotus townsendi* 3 7/8 · 1 3/4 (98-46)
Medium-sized bat, grayish brown in color with blackish wings, limbs, and tail membranes and large ears. Large

lumps between eyes and nostrils are distinctive. Occurs near caves, cliffs, and abandoned mines throughout much of the Pacific Northwest.

PALLID BAT *Antrozous pallidus* 4 3/4 · 1 7/8 (120-48)
Large yellowish or light brownish bat with buffy or whitish under parts. Membranes and ears are brownish. Occurs in river canyons in the semi-arid and desert areas in Oregon, western Idaho, and the Okanagan Valley of southeastern British Columbia.

BRAZILIAN FREE-TAILED BAT *Tadarida brasiliensis* 3 1/2 · 1 1/2 (90-39)
A medium-sized brownish bat with most of the tail free of the interfemoral membrane. Occurs in semi-arid areas, frequently old buildings and dwellings in southwestern Oregon.

BIG FREE-TAILED BAT *Tadarida molossa* 5 3/16 · 2 (133-51)
A large brownish bat with black ears and wing and tail membranes and the tail mostly free of the interfemoral membrane. Usually occurs in desert areas within its normal range, but has been recorded once in the Northwest in the New Westminster area of southwestern British Columbia, indicating the possible straying powers of winged animals.

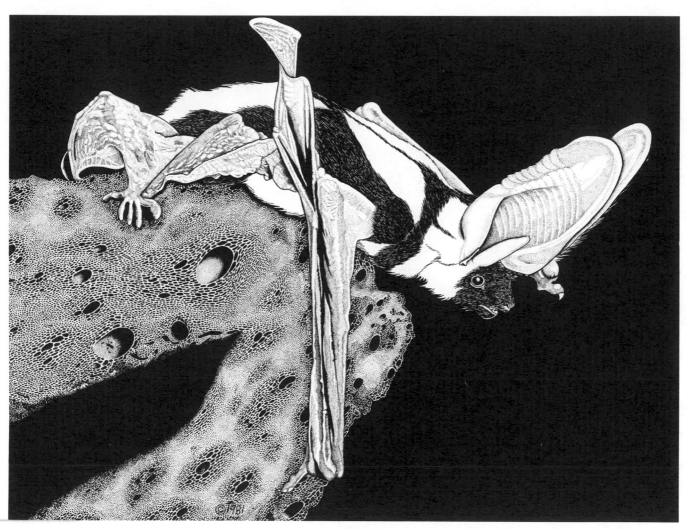

Spotted Bat

Common Pika

28

PIKAS

Rockslide at Packrat Gorge, habitat of the Common Pika and Bushy-tailed Wood Rat (Upper Priest Lake country, Washington; E.J.L.)

Campers and hikers in the timberless sub-alpine and alpine regions of the high mountains are likely to become acquainted with this small mammal during the cooler parts of the day by its peculiar short squeal or cry. Further evidence of the animal's presence is the occurrence of haystacks or forage piles in the cracks and crevices of the rockslides. If the weather is warm and sunny, these piles of harvest vegetation will sometimes be placed out in the open for drying, but are usually best cured in the shade of some over-hanging rock.

The boulders at the foot of cliffs provide the necessary openings in which these animals live and store their food. Pikas are diurnal and active throughout the year. They seldom venture more than several hundred feet from the shelter of their rocky homes. In these excursions, they generally remain on the rockslides. However, when they are gathering food for storage, they will venture away from the slide into the neighboring meadows and woods. These trips are made in the form of quick little runs, as though in fear of being too long away from the protection of the rocks. This caution is necessary because they are very vulnerable to attacks from predators. The Pikas' coloring and freezing behavior provide excellent means of defense. They run through the galleries in the rocks aided by the fur padding on their feet which enables them to leap from rock to rock without losing their footing or suffering undue abrasion from the rough surfaces. Each animal has its own territory within the colony. It will have three to five pathways leading to the central nest and other pathways to the haystacks. Family units will share one central nest in some instances. During the short summers of the alpine country, the Pika spends most of its time in gathering food for the long winter months. The animal holds the food cross-wise in the mouth while carrying it from the supply source to the haystacks. These piles are located in crevices in the talus and are so situated that they will be protected from rain and snow during the winter. The haystacks are inter-connected by well-beaten paths which may even extend to neighboring slides. These stacks have been found to contain as many as 34 different varieties of plants. Among these are grasses, thistles, and legumes. Thistles are often found in stacks and seem to be a favorite food.

Larrison: WASHINGTON MAMMALS

NORTHWEST SPECIES

COLLARED PIKA *Ochotona collaris* 7 1/2 - 5/8 (190-15) Upper parts grayish brown to grayish with a pale band on each side of the neck, nape, and shoulders (the "collar"). Ears with blackish edging. Under parts whitish. Rockslides in extreme northwestern British Columbia. Considered by some workers to be conspecific with the following form.

COMMON PIKA *Ochotona princeps* 8 1/8 - 5/8 (203-15) Upper parts light to dark brownish, often with blackish wash. Ears with white edges. Under parts yellowish. Rockslides and boulder areas at or near timberline in the mountains of the Northwest (except Olympics, Coast Ranges, southwestern Idaho mountains, and Vancouver Island). In certain lava beds areas in eastern Oregon and southern Idaho.

Common Pika (Dallas Hake)

Stored "hay" (Sunrise, Mt. Rainier, Washington; J.R.C.)

Pika haystack (central Cascades of Washington; E.J.L.)

A "peekaboo" Pika (Sunrise, Mt. Rainier; J.R.C.)

RABBITS AND HARES

White-tailed Jackrabbit

The native leporids of the Pacific Northwest may be assembled in two groups, the rabbits and hares. The rabbits are smaller members of the family, usually construct burrows in the earth, and are born in a less advanced condition than are their larger, surface-inhabiting, and more fully developed cousins.

Four species of rabbits occur in our region.

The diminutive Pygmy Rabbit is a denizen of the dense sagebrush stands of our northern steppe deserts where it is seldom seen by the average citizen. In its favored haunts, however, it can frequently be approached closely and when flushed, will seldom run more than a few yards. It may be readily identified by its obvious lack of a white "cottontail" and small size. This rabbit is

31

Nuttall's Cottontail

Nuttall's Cottontail (Mammoth Hot Springs, Yellowstone National Park; J.R.C.)

Of the three native Northwest hares, the medium-sized Snowshoe Hare seems to be in the best environmental shape, as it is strictly an inhabitant of the coniferous forests, a vegetational type that is well represented in the region, particularly in the mountainous and coastal areas. The dark-colored non-varying coastal race, *L. a. washingtoni,* has probably suffered considerable reduction in numbers as a result of the urban sprawl in the Puget Sound area. Of the two jackrabbits, things also have in general been "tough" with the exception of a few places, as in southeastern Idaho where the Black-tailed Jackrabbit reached epidemic numbers in the winter of 1981-82 to the point where extreme measures had to be adopted in their control to save the stacked hay crop and other forage. The reduction of the sagebrush plains caused by converting much land to irrigated cash crops and dry land wheat farming, as in the Columbia Basin of Washington, has greatly reduced their numbers elsewhere. In the "old days", an automobile trip across the Basin would reveal hundreds of crushed jacks along the highway. Now, a similar trip will seldom produce a single one. More strongly endangered is the larger White-tailed Jackrabbit which prefers the more grassy higher ranges above the sagebrush and below the woodlands and timber of the mountains in the dry

threatened with extirpation in many parts of its range in the Northwest, as the sagebrush areas are progressively "reclaimed" and the brush removed. In fact, outside of the forest-dwelling Snowshoe Hare, most of the region's rabbit and hare fauna may suffer from habitat alteration. These animals are particularly vulnerable, as herbivores go, due to their relatively large size as compared with the more successful smaller rodents.

The Brush Rabbit inhabits brushy places in western Oregon in our region and is a rather dull-colored species. It, too, lacks a cottontail. The increased occupation of lowland areas in its range may spell difficulties for this species, also. It lives in a somewhat marginal environment and such habitats are in danger.

The native Nuttall's Cottontail has been joined in some parts of the Northwest by the introduced Eastern Cottontail. The two are very difficult to separate, especially in the field. Both may be identified readily by the white "cottontail", which is particularly obvious when the animals are running away from one. Cottontails inhabit a variety of rocky broken habitats and seem quite able to fend for themselves in close proximity to mankind. In fact, they do well in parks, college campuses, and even in the backyards of residential areas, in spite of the plethora of domestic cats and dogs in such places.

Snowshoe Hare (Naches, Washington; Lee Paulinsky)

33

Black-tailed Jackrabbit

country. With the conversion of much of this vegetational type to agriculture and grazing, the beautiful "white-tail" is now seldom seen.

NORTHWEST SPECIES

PYGMY RABBIT *Brachylagus idahoensis* 10 5/16 · 1 (270-25)
A small rabbit, grizzled gray above and pale buffy white below. Silvery gray in winter. The tail is short and not a white fluff as in cottontails. Dense sagebrush and greasewood as

well as sand dune areas in southcentral Washington, eastern and central Oregon, and south and central Idaho.

BRUSH RABBIT *Sylvilagus bachmani* 13 3/8 · 1 1/8 (340-30)
Medium-sized rabbit with dark brownish upper parts and light brownish or buffy gray under parts. No cottontail present. Brushy places in lowlands, especially near water, in western Oregon.

EASTERN COTTONTAIL *Sylvilagus floridanus* 15 · 1 1/2 (382-38)
Upper parts brownish with tan-colored lower back and

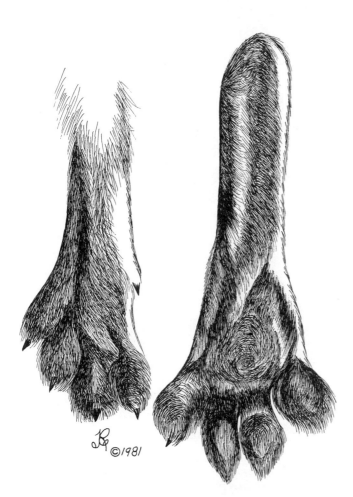

Snowshoe Hare feet (left, fore foot; right, hind foot)

rump. Ears darker than back. Under parts white, though sometimes pale cinnamon, resembling sides. Inside of ears whitish. Wears the obvious cottontail. Brushy weedy places, swamps, and broken habitats in southwestern British Columbia, eastern and western Washington, and western Oregon. Introduced.

NUTTALL'S COTTONTAIL *Sylvilagus nuttalli* 13 3/16 · 1 3/4 (340-45)
Grizzled grayish with yellowish cast on upper parts and whitish below. Obvious cottontail. Edges of ears tinged with white or buffy on inside and blackish on outside. Difficult to separate on external characters from the Eastern Cottontail. Sagebrush, rocky canyons, dry gullies, brush, orchards, etc., in eastern Washington and Oregon, western and southern Idaho, and the Okanagan Valley of British Columbia.

SNOWSHOE HARE *Lepus americanus* 17 · 1 1/2 (430-38)

A medium-sized hare, brownish above and whitish below in summer and white (with dark ear tips) in winter, except in the lowlands west of the Cascades where it becomes only slightly paler. The hind feet are relatively quite large, especially appearing so in winter. Coniferous forests throughout most of the Northwest.

WHITE-TAILED JACKRABBIT *Lepus townsendi* 23 · 3 1/8 (585-80)
A large hare, grayish above and whitish below (with white tail) in summer and pure white (dark ear tips) in winter. Grasslands and grassy sagebrush in eastern Washington, eastern Oregon, Idaho, and the Okanagan Valley of British Columbia. Range much reduced over former distribution.

BLACK-TAILED JACKRABBIT *Lepus californicus* 21 · 3 1/4 (535-82)
Grizzled grayish brown above and buffy white below. Ears tipped with black and tail with black band on upper surface. Sagebrush and adjacent grass and hay fields in eastern Washington, eastern and southwestern Oregon, and southern Idaho.

EUROPEAN RABBIT *Oryctolagus cuniculus* 16 1/4 · 3 1/8 (445-80)
Reddish brown to dark grayish and brownish or whitish on belly. Ears relatively short. Introduced and common on San Juan and some other islands of the San Juan group of Washington.

A Black-tailed Jackrabbit's form, its only home (Cassia Co., Idaho; E.J.L.)

Mountain Beaver

MOUNTAIN BEAVERS

Sewellel (*Haplodon rufus*) is a name given by the natives to a small animal found in the timbered country on this coast. It is more abundant in the neighborhood of the Great Falls and rapids of the Columbia than on the coast which we inhabit. The natives make great use of the skins of this animal in forming their robes, which they dress with the fur on, and attach them together with sinews of the elk or deer. The skin, when dressed, is from 14 to 18 inches long and from 7 to 9 in width. The tail is always separated from the skin by the natives when making their robes [the tail is a mere stump, which the natives would hardly take the trouble to remove, and which Captain Lewis overlooked]. This animal mounts a tree and burrows in the ground, precisely like a squirrel. The ears are short, thin, pointed, and covered with a fine short hair, of a uniform reddish brown; at the bottom or base of the long hairs, which exceed the fur but little in length, as well as the fur itself, are of a dark color next to the skin for two-thirds of their length. Of this animal the fur and hair are very fine, short, thickly set and silky; the ends of the fur and tips of the hair are of a reddish brown, and that color predominates in the usual appearance of the animal. Captain Lewis offered considerable awards to the Indians, but was never able to procure one of those animals alive. (Lewis and Clark)

The sewellel is one of the most remarkable animals discovered by Lewis and Clark. Fortunately they gave it a name by which it could be called, and which has passed into our language. I put it in the Century Dictionary in the form in which it here occurs, and which therefore may be accepted as the correct spelling. It will be observed that Captain Lewis never saw the animal itself, but only the robes made of its skin by the natives. It seems by the later researches of George Gibbs into the unspellable jargon of the Columbia River Indians, that "sewellel" is their name for the robes, mistaken by Captain Lewis for the name of the animal which furnishes the skin, and that the latter is "show'tl" in Nisqually. The animal is about the size of a muskrat, and of

Alder bottom habitat of the Mountain Beaver (Snohomish Co., Washington; E.J.L.)

much the same color; in fact, it greatly resembles a muskrat minus the long scaly tail and without webbed feet. (Elliott Coues)

The Journals of Lewis and Clark
(Coues Ed.)

* * *

The Mountain Beaver, the name by which it is universally known at present, is a unique Pacific Northwest mammal, lone surviving representative of an ancient primitive rodent family and thus what is often referred to as a living fossil. Although persecuted for its burrowing and tree seedling destroying habits, let us hope that it never joins the growing list of extinct North American animal species.

NORTHWEST SPECIES

MOUNTAIN BEAVER *Aplodontia rufa* 14 - 1 1/2 (350-38) A stout chunky rodent the size of a rabbit or small woodchuck with blackish-brown fur and usually a white spot behind the ear. Head round and short and claws on fore feet long and straight. Moist open woods, alder bottoms, and bracken fern jungles, west of the Cascades crest in the Northwest.

Townsend's Chipmunk

CHIPMUNKS

Log piles, favorite habitat of chipmunks (Wenas Cr., Yakima Co., Washington; E.J.L.)

Chipmunks, the smallest [Pacific Northwest] squirrels are bright, active, vociferous, diurnal rodents with a series of alternating light and dark stripes over the back and upper sides running from the shoulders to the rump. The sides of the head are similarly striped and the lower sides are plain colored and of the same hue as the central portion of the undersurface of the tail. The bellies are white or buffy. The size of our chipmunks is about halfway between that of a mouse and a rat. Chipmunks are restricted to coniferous forests or brush, hibernate during the winter months, and are active during daylight hours, mostly on sunny days. Unlike many of their squirrel relatives, chipmunks spend most of their time on the ground or in low bushes and seldom climb trees. They are not found in the open habitats preferred by the ground squirrels....

While most chipmunks prefer forests or heavy brush areas, the Least Chipmunk is a devotee of sagebrush [except for some races elsewhere than Washington which are to be found in open timber]. To see these grayish mites, one must go to their habitat and search carefully for them. The author [Larrison] has seen most of the "sagebrush chipmunks" he has studied in Washington in the barren sage hills between Vantage and Ellensburg. In walking through the brush, one occasionally observes the flash of a little grayish animal as it scurries from the protection of one bush to that of another. They are not vocal and sight reveals most of them. In specimen collecting, the biologist gets the majority of his specimens with mouse traps baited with dry rolled oats....

Campers and hikers in the sub-alpine parks

39

Yellow Pine Chipmunk

and pine slopes of the state soon make acquaintance with this small, agile, brightly-colored chipmunk [the Yellow Pine Chipmunk]. Curious, vociferous, and not adverse to stealing food scraps about the camp, this little sprite is abundant in the open coniferous forests of the upper parts of the mountains and in the yellow pine woods of the intermediate areas of the eastern part of Washington. It may be identified by its habitat, small size, and bright colors. No other chipmunk occurs within its ecologic range. The Yellow Pine Chipmunk is a noisy fellow and its presence is soon made evident to the invader of its brushy domain....

This species is something more of a tree climber than are the other chipmunks, although its arboreal excursions are limited mostly to the smaller pines and firs and it seldom ascends much above 10 or 15 feet. Seeds, other vegetational material, and some insects make up most of the diet of this species. In captivity, it will accept peanuts, rolled oats, sunflower seeds, dried bread crusts, cantaloupe rinds, and meat scraps. The nest is usually placed at the end of a short burrow a few feet in length or in a small cave or crevice in rocks. A favorite spot is in the cracks or narrow clefts in spalling granite if vegetation is nearby. The food caches are placed in the nest burrow or chamber. Mating is done in April with the young born some 30-40 days later in May or June. Five to seven young chipmunks constitute a litter of which only one is raised a year. The young are naked, blind, and helpless. Though without fur, the dorsal stripe pattern is revealed by dark streaks of pigment in the skin of the back of these infants. They are weaned some six weeks later and appear outside as two-thirds grown animals with a thinner fur and duller color pattern

Habitat of the Townsend's Ground Squirrel (foreground) and the Yellow Pine Chipmunk and Cascade Mantled Ground Squirrel (forest in background) (Wenas Creek, Yakima Co., Washington; E.J.L.)

Habitat of the sagebrush form of the Least Chipmunk (Owyhee Desert, Idaho; E.J.L.)

than those of the adults. They will retain this pattern until the spring molt. By the end of the summer, the young are almost as large as the adults....

Yellow Pine Chipmunks occur in non-agricultural areas — almost entirely in forested regions — so seldom come in conflict with man's economy. It is true that they may garner a few seeds from barn, forest, or garden, but their attractiveness as a part of the wild fauna, their confiding ways, and their contribution to the food base of carnivores make them a valuable part of the natural scene without which the life of the outdoor enthusiast would be a little drab....

As one walks down a trail in some dense fir forest in the Puget Sound country, he may be greeted by a sharp *kwiss* from a nearby brush patch in a small clearing or burn. If our observer remains motionless and does a little lip-squeaking, he will soon see a dark brownish chipmunk climb slowly out on some half-exposed branch to look the situation over. Phlegmatic in behavior and preferring to keep well within vegetational cover, the Townsend's Chipmunk is the only member of the genus in the thickly forested regions of Western Washington and the Cascade Mountains. This fact, plus the relatively large size and dark coloration [the lowland race having no dorsal light stripes] make the identification of this species easy. It is not nearly as common in its range as the other species are in theirs and is more often heard than seen.

Larrison: WASHINGTON MAMMALS

NORTHWEST SPECIES

LEAST CHIPMUNK *Eutamias minimus* 7 1/2 - 3 3/8 (190-85)
Small, grayish, or yellowish chipmunk most often seen in open country sagebrush east of the Cascade Mountains or in open woods in eastern Idaho.

YELLOW PINE CHIPMUNK *Eutamias amoenus* 8 3/4 - 3 15/16 (223-101)
Medium-sized brightly-colored chipmunk with sharply contrasting light and dark stripes on the back. Open to semi-open coniferous forests of the subalpine areas and the yellow pine woods of the mountains of the Pacific Northwest.

TOWNSEND'S CHIPMUNK *Eutamias townsendi* 10 1/3 - 4 3/5 (258-115)
Large dark-colored chipmunk with brownish light dorsal stripes and dark brownish sides. The dense coniferous forests of the Coast, Olympic, and Cascade Mountains.

Habitat of the Cliff Chipmunk (Silent City of Rocks, Cassia Co., Idaho; E.J.L.)

YELLOW-CHEEKED CHIPMUNK: REDWOOD CHIPMUNK *Eutamias ochrogenys* 10 2/5 · 4 1/2 (265-115)
Similar to the Townsend's Chipmunk but has reddish-yellow under parts. Redwood forest areas of southwestern Oregon.

ALLEN'S CHIPMUNK *Eutamias senex* 9 1/2 · 4 (242-102)
Medium-sized chipmunk; grayer and smaller than typical Townsend's Chipmunk. Upper parts with brownish and light gray stripes, sides reddish brown, and belly whitish. Yellow

pine and lodgepole pine forests on the east slopes of the southern Cascades in Oregon.

SISKIYOU CHIPMUNK *Eutamias siskiyou* 10 · 4 1/3 (255-110)
Large chipmunk with one black, four brown, and four gray stripes on back; grayish brown sides; and light yellow under parts. Pine woods of the Siskiyou and Rogue River Mountains of southwestern Oregon.

CLIFF CHIPMUNK *Eutamias dorsalis* 8 1/4 · 3 5/8 (210-91)
Medium-sized grayish chipmunk with very indistinct stripes on the back and bright red under surface of the tail. Rocky juniper and pinyon pine groves in extreme southern Idaho.

RED-TAILED CHIPMUNK *Eutamias ruficaudus* 9 1/4 · 4 3/8 (235-110)
Large dark-colored chipmunk with bright red sides and tail, contrasting dorsal stripes, and conspicuous white belly. Dense coniferous forests of the Okanogan Highlands, Selkirks, and Bitterroots of northeastern Washington and northern Idaho, southeastern British Columbia, and western Montana.

UINTA CHIPMUNK *Eutamias umbrinus* 9 · 4 (230-100)
Large drab-colored chipmunk with brownish-gray sides, grayish head and rump, and broad blackish dark dorsal stripes. Semi-open coniferous timber in mountains of southeastern corner of Idaho.

Woodchuck

MARMOTS

The Cascade hoary marmot is one of the largest rodents in North America. It is principally, if not exclusively, diurnal and excavates large burrows, sometimes on grassy meadows, more often among the boulders of a rock slide. The burrows may be single or in colonies connected by well-beaten paths. Dr. C. Hart Merriam writes that occasionally runways are found extending from the rock slides several hundred feet to favorite feeding grounds, and it is of interest to note that these marmot runways serve as highways for several other mammals also, such as chipmunks, conies, meadow mice, and white-footed mice.

The masses of slide rock resulting from the effect of frost and ice on the cliffs furnish the marmot's best protection. When away from his stony shelter the animal appears nervous, but on regaining the rocks his anxiety largely disappears. He is accustomed to remain in one position for several minutes. Usually this is a ruglike attitude on a flat rock. Sampson writes that in many cases the surface of the marmots' lookout rock has become quite polished from its use by many succeeding generations of watchers and suggests that St. Simeon Stylites himself was hardly more constant. (Sierra Club Bulletin, vol. 6, 1908, p. 37). Occasionally the marmot assumes the posture of the recumbent lion of the conventional gateway. If

Olympic Marmot (J.W.T.)

startled he often sits up on his haunches, diving out of sight, if close to his burrow, on the near approach of danger. If thoroughly alarmed he does not reappear for hours....

The marmot's food consists exclusively of green vegetation. Grasses, composite flowers (*Arnica* and *Agoseris*), green leaves, and blue lupines have been found in stomachs examined. Cantwell observes that the animal seldom stops to eat on his foraging expeditions, but carries mouthfuls of green stuff back into his den, where it is consumed in safety. Early morning and late

Hoary Marmot (Frozen Lake, Mt. Rainier; J.R.C.)

Yellow-bellied Marmot (Painted Rocks near Yakima, Washington; J.R.C.)

Hoary Marmot

Alpine habitat of the Hoary Marmot (Lake of the Crags, Teton National Park, Wyoming; J.R.C.)

afternoon are favorite times for feeding. No evidence of storage of vegetation for winter use has been obtained.

If one invades an amphitheater-like cirque inhabited by marmots, his appearance is immediately proclaimed to all the wilderness people by a clear and penetrating whistle, a sound possessing a distinctly musical quality, and under favorable conditions carrying for more than a mile. Often one individual apparently assumes the role of watchman or guardian, locating himself on some high rock and giving the alarm on the approach of anything of a suspicious nature. The whistle is really a squeal made in the throat, the lips of course, taking no direct part in the sound production. Ordinarily a single note is given, but one heard on Burroughs Mountain whistled five times in rapid succession; one at Success Cleaver whistled at intervals of three or four seconds; and one observed in Paradise Valley by Dr. C. Hart

Merriam in 1897 repeated the whistled note one hundred times a minute, loud and clear, at first, but after the animal had kept it up without any rest or interval for a half hour it decreased somewhat in strength and frequency, falling to 94, 92, and finally 90 a minute. It seemed to be an inspiratory whistle, and his sides drew in with every note. It appeared to be very fatiguing....

Among enemies of the marmot probably the coyote and timber wolf are most important. The black bear may also take toll of their numbers, and the golden eagle is much feared. Slight attention is paid to hawks, however, even when the young are about.

Taylor and Shaw: MAMMALS AND BIRDS of
RAINIER NATIONAL PARK

NORTHWEST SPECIES

EASTERN WOODCHUCK *Marmota monax* 21 1/3 · 5 (541-127)
A small dark marmot with cinnamon brown upper parts [frosted with white-tipped hairs], reddish brown under parts, and a relatively unmarked face. Meadows, rockslides, and woodlands in northeastern Washington, northern Idaho, and eastern and central British Columbia. Not common.

YELLOW-BELLIED MARMOT *Marmota flaviventris* 23 1/4 · 6 3/4 (590-170)
Large marmot with grizzled dark grayish upper parts, yellowish or reddish under parts, and a strongly marked black and white face. Widespread in rockslides and rocky outcroppings in the Northwest east of the Cascades.

HOARY MARMOT *Marmota caligata* 30 · 8 5/8 (750-220)
Large grayish marmot with dusky gray sides, black feet, and strongly marked face. Rocky areas in the subalpine zone of the Cascades (except Oregon) and the Rockies.

OLYMPIC MARMOT *Marmota olympus* 28 · 8 (714-204)
Drab brownish marmot grizzled with white and with considerable white on face. Rocky places in subalpine areas of the Olympic Mountains.

VANCOUVER MARMOT *Marmota vancouverensis* 26 1/2 · 8 5/8 (675-220)
Dark brownish marmot with grizzled white hairs on back, white spots on belly, and a grayish patch on the muzzle. High mountain areas on Vancouver Island.

Golden Mantled Ground Squirrel

GROUND SQUIRRELS

Some 30 years ago, the author [Larrison] live-trapped a young Golden-mantled Ground Squirrel near Stevens Pass [Washington]. "Stevie", as the squirrel was called, soon became a pet of the family. Housed in a large hardware cloth cage and well provided with food, water, and cotton for bedding, this mammal remained a part of the family for 11 years, before dying in hibernation. Stevie made a fine pet and had many interesting habits and behavior mannerisms. Placed outside in the backyard each day during the summer, it made an excellent watch dog, notifying us whenever a neighbor's cat strayed too close. During the early and middle of the summer, life for the squirrel was easy and carefree. Only enough food was taken to satisfy the hunger of the moment. The nest was trampled into a mat during the day and was only loosely pulled together in the evening to form a bed. With the advent of the first high fogs in early August in the Seattle area, much of

Stevie's behavior changed. Life became more serious. Food gathering and storage were the order of the day. Stevie would take as many peanuts as would be offered to it, carefully removing the outer husks and brownish skin and depositing the kernels in the back corner of the cage under the nest. Many of the nuts fell through the wire screen of the cage bottom, to be retrieved by the author and offered again to the squirrel. Stevie didn't care; it would re-store them. Sometimes, half a pound of peanuts would keep Stevie busy all morning.

Stevie became more business-like and less easy going in early autumn. Particular attention was paid to improving and enlarging the nest. Handfuls of cotton that were placed inside the cage would be torn up into bundles of fibers and stuffed into its mouth until a hard cotton pellet would be formed. These pellets would then be placed together to form a domed nest chamber

Columbian Ground Squirrel

Townsend's Ground Squirrel (Yakima, Washington; J.R.C.)

Washington Ground Squirrel (Scootenay Reservoir, Franklin Co., Washington; J.R.C.)

Columbian Ground Squirrel (Lake Mistaya, Jasper National Park, Alberta; J.R.C.)

with a hole in one side. The roots of grass would be pulled up through the half-inch mesh floor and incorporated into the nest walls. The first dark rainy weather in mid-September would reduce Stevie's activities to a few hours and finally (it was kept in the basement by now) to an hour or so a day. Some days, it would not come out of the nest at all. Finally, the squirrel was "in" for the winter. Not completely, however. A few hours of bright, sunny, windy weather between warm and cold fronts in winter would bring Stevie out for a short look around, though we could never see that it ate or drank anything at such times. Stevie emerged from winter sleep in April, depending on the warmness and brightness of the weather. Several times, the author brought the still torpid squirrel into a warm room and placed it on a table. After a few minutes, the animal began to twitch. The shaking increased until the entire body was moving, particularly the legs. The rigidness of the body disappeared, it slowly began to straighten out, and the animal crouched in a prone position, breathing heavily. Finally, it became completely alert with an interest in food and water. One could not help wondering whether this awakening process was a painful one.

Stevie taught us many things — the problems it had and how it solved them. There is much we could learn from our wild brothers, if we could but come to know them better. Such is the message of Stevie's story....

The open parts of the lowlands and intermediate elevations of the extreme eastern part of Washington are populated by hordes of Columbian Ground Squirrels, large, grayish, speckle-backed rodents. They prefer a variety of habitats ranging from open wheatfields and scabrock to yellow pine woods and, occasionally, sub-alpine meadows. They appear in early April and re-enter dormancy at the lower elevations in mid to late July. Columbians are slow-moving fat fellows without the grace of a tree squirrel or the vivacity of a chipmunk. Poisoned, shot, gassed, run over, plowed out, and eaten by coyotes and hawks, they nevertheless are a numerous and prominent part of the mammal picture in their native haunts and provide some activity along otherwise monotonous highways.

This species was intensively studied by the

late William T. Shaw when he was mammalogist and ornithologist at Washington State University. His papers reveal the careful research he performed to uncover the many facts of the life history of these big squirrels. Small in stature and badly crippled, Professor Shaw became famous as an authority on Northwest mammals. His studies of alpine species in the Cascades were important break-throughs in early 20th century ornithology and mammalogy in Washington state. He worked out the life history and ecologic distribution of the Hepburn's Rosy Finch and the Bog Lemming in the Mount Baker area. The author [Larrison] once commented to Professor Shaw about the difficulties of studying Arctic-Alpine birds and mammals, particularly by so disabled a person. Shaw's reply still rings in his ears and the author has repeated it several times to discouraged graduate students: "Where there's a will, there's a way." Even if it involved being carried up mountain peaks on the shoulders of football players!

The east-west course of the Columbia River where it separates Washington and Oregon has provided an important barrier to the northward range extension of many mammals. One of these was the California Ground Squirrel, a large sciurid very common in the California valley area. Some squirrels got across the river in 1912 and established a colony at Bingen and were at White

Arctic Ground Squirrel (northern British Columbia; E.J.L.)

California Ground Squirrel (Cottonwood Cr., Yakima Co., Washington; J.R.C.)

Salmon by 1915. First the Klickitat area was populated. Later, the crest of the Simcoe Mountains was passed and the invasion continued northward along the lower, intermediate, east slopes of the Cascades. Here, the squirrels have come to occupy a zone between the yellow pine haunts of the Golden-mantled Ground Squirrel and the arid domain of the Townsend's. Northward extension has been reported as far as the Naches area and lower Wenas Creek and Umptanum areas. It will be interesting to see how far this rapid range extension will go, especially if it should swing around the northern fringe of the Columbia Basin and bring the California and Columbian Ground Squirrels together. What an interesting competition that might be!

The author [Larrison] and a companion sat beside their car near a small grassy flat a few miles north of Connell in eastern Washington. We had come to search for Washington's Ground Squirrels. None was in sight. Every so often, a thin bird-like whistle was heard, so soft and formless that it could not be detected unless one were straining his ears for it. Even when heard, the location of the source was nearly impossible to determine. Such were the warning notes of

White-tailed Antelope Squirrel

Washington's Ground Squirrels on that March day in 1957.

This species is of interest in that it is one of the derivatives of the basic Townsend's Ground Squirrel stock. From the original group, probably located in the Great Basin, numerous populations expanded to radiate into the arid extensions of the Great Basin desert. Barriers appeared breaking off segments of this once-joined stock. Subsequent evolution and adaptation in position produced a number of races and, where barrierization and resulting divergence were sufficiently marked, separate species were formed, as in the case of the Washington Ground Squirrel and the Idaho Spotted Ground Squirrel. The history of the Townsend's Ground Squirrel complex in the Pacific Northwest provides some excellent lessons in zoogeography.

Larrison: WASHINGTON MAMMALS

NORTHWEST SPECIES

WHITE-TAILED ANTELOPE SQUIRREL *Ammospermophilus leucurus* 8 1/4 - 2 3/16 (210-56)
Small ground squirrel with dark grayish upper parts, white line in dark of upper sides, white belly, and a short tail (dark above, white below) carried up over the rump to show the white undersurface. Open dry habitats in southeastern Oregon and southern Idaho.

Uinta Ground Squirrel (Wyoming; J.R.C.)

TOWNSEND'S GROUND SQUIRREL *Spermophilus townsendi* 8 7/8 · 2 (225-50)
Small buffy-gray ground squirrel with pale dots on back and sides, reddish buff face and legs, and pale buffy under parts. Sagebrush, grass, and weeds in eastern Oregon, southern Idaho, and southeastern Washington west of the Columbia River.

WASHINGTON GROUND SQUIRREL *Spermophilus washingtoni* 9 1/6 · 2 (229-50)
Similar to the Townsend's Ground Squirrel but darker with strongly dotted upper parts. Southeastern Washington, east of the Columbia River, and northeastern Oregon.

IDAHO GROUND SQUIRREL *Spermophilus brunneus* 8 1/2 · 1 7/8 (215-48)
Similar to the Townsend's Ground Squirrel, but darker (brownish, rather than buffy gray) and with light brownish under parts and white chin. Westcentral Idaho.

ELEGANT GROUND SQUIRREL *Spermophilus elegans* 12 1/8 · 3 5/16 (308-85)
Medium-sized, plain-backed, unstriped ground squirrel with a buffy wash over grayish back and sides and a pale yellow under surface of the tail. Parts of southern Idaho and southeastern Oregon.

UINTA GROUND SQUIRREL *Spermophilus armatus* 11 3/4 · 3 (300-76)
Medium-sized, unstriped, plain-backed ground squirrel with grayish head and shoulders and grayish-brown back and sides. Undersurface of tail is grayish. Meadows, pastures, and fields in eastern Idaho.

BELDING'S GROUND SQUIRREL *Spermophilus beldingi* 11 · 2 9/16 (282-66)
Medium-sized, plain-backed, unstriped ground squirrel with

grayish upper parts washed with pinkish down the center of the back and chestnut brown under surface of the tail. Open country in southwestern Idaho and eastern Oregon.

COLUMBIAN GROUND SQUIRREL *Spermophilus columbianus* 14 · 3 7/8 (368-98)
A large spotted or speckled grayish to light brownish ground squirrel with a brownish or yellowish face and buffy to grayish under parts. Under surface of tail is dark with gray-tipped hairs. Interior of the Northwest: east, north, and south of the Columbia Basin.

ARCTIC GROUND SQUIRREL *Spermophilus parryi* 15 7/8 · 4 1/2 (400-115)
Large ground squirrel similar to the Columbian Ground

Golden Mantled Ground Squirrel (Wallowa Mts., Oregon; J.R.C.)

Cascade Mantled Ground Squirrel (Sunrise, Mt. Rainier, Washington; J.R.C.)

Squirrel but more brownish and with tawny sides and under parts. Open places in northern British Columbia.

ROCK SQUIRREL *Spermophilus variegatus* 20-9 (510-230)
Large ground squirrel with dark grayish to blackish upper parts and long bushy tail. Extreme southeastern Idaho.

CALIFORNIA GROUND SQUIRREL *Spermophilus beecheyi* 18 1/3 · 8 (458-200)
Large dark-colored ground squirrel with grayish nape, dark longitudinal band on back, and grayish sides. Tail is long. Western Oregon and southcentral Washington.

GOLDEN MANTLED GROUND SQUIRREL *Spermophilus lateralis* 9 5/8 · 3 1/2 (245-90)
Chipmunk-like but much larger. Black and white stripes on sides of back (the back plain and brownish) with golden or light brownish head and shoulders. Open woodlands, brush, and rimrock in Idaho, much of Oregon, and northeastern and southeastern Washington.

CASCADE MANTLED GROUND SQUIRREL *Spermophilus saturatus* 11 3/4 · 4 1/10 (300-105)
Very similar to the Golden Mantled Ground Squirrel, but

Eastern Gray Squirrel (Woodland Park, Seattle, Washington; J.R.C.)

darker and more drab, without bright mantle and strongly contrastive lateral stripes. Cascade Mountains of Washington and southern British Columbia.

TREE SQUIRRELS

Western Gray Squirrel

Five species of tree squirrels are to be found in the Pacific Northwest. Two of these, the Eastern Gray Squirrel and the Fox Squirrel, have been introduced from the eastern part of the United States and enjoy restricted toe-holds only in several parts of our region. The more numerous of the two, the Eastern Gray Squirrel, is mainly in parks and residential areas in certain of the larger cities and has shown little or no intention to invade the wilder less populated parts.

A most handsome member of the tree squirrel entourage is the Western Gray Squirrel, a large, totally gray, bushy-tailed squirrel. Unfortunately, this species is rather strongly restricted, being found mostly in the open woods below the southern end of Puget Sound in Washington and

Red Squirrel

in oak woodlands along the eastern base of the Cascades and similar habitat in Oregon. Most widely ranging in the Northwest of the large squirrels are the chickarees — the Eastern Red Squirrel and the Douglas's Squirrel. Somewhat similar in appearance, they may be separated by the smaller size of the Douglas's and the fact that its undersides are yellowish or orangy while those of the Red Squirrel are white. The distributional ranges in the Northwest are quite different, though they meet in the northern part of the east slope of the Cascades in Washington. Some hybridization has been found and it has been suggested that the two are conspecific. Anyone who knows the Douglas's Squirrel well would not follow this, however, as the habits, behavior, appearance, and voice of the two chickarees are noticeably different. What does it matter if there may be a similarity of penis bone or zygomatic arch or even chromosome number between groups of mammals? It is the respective ecologic niches with the resultant adaptation to such niches that should be considered as characterizing taxa. Kipling well put it when he wrote:

> For the Colonel's Lady an' Judy O'Grady
> Are sisters under their skins!

NORTHWEST SPECIES

EASTERN GRAY SQUIRREL *Sciurus carolinensis* 18 4/5 · 9 (480-230)
A large, grayish, bushy-tailed tree squirrel with whitish under parts and long white-tipped hairs on the tail. Completely black melanistic individuals sometimes occur. Introduced to various urban areas in the region, as Seattle, Spokane, and Vancouver, British Columbia.

FOX SQUIRREL *Sciurus niger* 20 7/8 · 9 (530-230)
A large, bushy-tailed, reddish-gray squirrel. Under parts orange or yellow. Ears, feet, and margins of tail reddish. Introduced in various parts of the Northwest, as Asotin, Seattle, and Okanogan, Washington; and Boise, Bruneau, Nampa, Weiser, Caldwell, Rupert, and Aberdeen, Idaho. Prefers urban areas, but also invades agricultural land.

WESTERN GRAY SQUIRREL *Sciurus griseus* 22 1/3 · 10 4/5 (570-270)
A large bushy-tailed tree squirrel with grizzled gray upper parts and pure white under parts. The back does not have the reddish overwash as does the Eastern Gray Squirrel. Tail blackish gray, edged with white. Oak and pine woods in western Oregon and southwestern and westcentral Washington.

RED SQUIRREL *Tamiasciurus hudsonicus* 12 1/2 · 5 (320-128)
Medium-sized tree squirrel with dark reddish or brownish upper parts and whitish under parts separated by a dark lateral line. Tail blackish. Coniferous forests of northeastern and extreme eastern Washington, northeastern Oregon, Idaho, and British Columbia.

DOUGLAS'S SQUIRREL *Tamiasciurus douglasi* 11 7/8 · 4 11/16 (306-120)
A medium-sized tree squirrel similar to the Red Squirrel but with orange or yellow under parts. Tail is blackish brown, edged with white or yellow. Coniferous forests of southwestern British Columbia, western Washington (includes all of the Cascades except the northeastern portion), and western and central Oregon (including the Cascades).

Red Squirrel (Rick Matthes)

Red Squirrel's cone shucking station and cache (left) (Pend Oreille Co., Washington; E.J.L.)

Northern Flying Squirrel

FLYING SQUIRRELS

These beautiful large-eyed, soft-furred squirrels are mainly nocturnal and hence are rarely seen and little known. Trappers find them in traps set for marten in the woods, woodchoppers see them as they soar away from falling trees in which they had their homes, and field naturalists get a few for specimens by setting traps on stumps, branches, or leaning trunks, and sometimes in old cabins and abandoned houses. They are never found far from timber and rarely on the ground. Their usual method of travel is to run up one tree and soar away to the next, always alighting at a lower level than the starting points.

Their holes and nests are generally in hollow trees and, where these are not available, in masses of moss or old leaf nests of other squirrels, or in moss and twig and leaf nests built by themselves in forks or branches of trees. At Gold Beach, McLellan found one occupying a small spherical nest of sticks and moss in the branches of a fir tree, and some of the many nests examined in the tops of conifers undoubtedly belong to them instead of other squirrels.

The females have four pairs of mammae — 1 inguinal, 2 abdominal, and 1 pectoral — and the young are probably 3 to 6 in number, as in closely related forms....

On rare occasions these squirrels get into attics, barns, or storehouses and do slight mischief, but generally they are scarce about buildings or in the open, where cats and owls prey upon them. Usually they are quite harmless and, although rarely seen, form an interesting feature of the forest wildlife.

The food, like that of all flying squirrels, is quite varied, as is shown by the different baits that attract them to traps — rolled oats, bread, biscuits, bacon, and the meat used for marten bait. They often gather around old campsites for the scattered grain and food scraps thrown out and seem to be rather omnivorous in their tastes. Cantwell picked up an interesting flying squirrel story near Wallowa Lake that has every indication of being authentic. In a log cabin back in the mountains where some old settlers resided, an old-fashioned spinning wheel was stored in the attic. This wheel was sometimes heard revolving at night when no one was near it and was often found still in motion when examined. The house finally acquired the reputation of being haunted until one brave member of the family stole silently up to the dark room when the whirring of the wheel was heard and with a flashlight saw one of these flying squirrels running on top of the wheel as it spun beneath the animal's skilled tread....

These large handsome flying squirrels [*Glaucomys sabrinus bullatus*] live in both the yellow pine timber, and higher up through the lodgepole pine and spruce forests, always among the tall trees where they travel through the air from trunk to trunk or come down the trunks to gather food on the ground. They rarely get far from trees, which are their main protection from enemies. Even the marten, which may follow them to the top of the tallest tree, is left behind as they soar away to distant trunks. The type and two others were caught in traps set for marten at the base of trees and baited with the bodies of birds and small mammals that had been skinned for specimens. The flying squirrels are always a great annoyance to trappers as they are fond of meat and constantly get into marten traps. They are rather omnivorous in taste and accept almost any

Pet flying squirrel (J.R.C.)

camp supplies, regularly visiting camp grounds for the scraps of food to be found. At the type locality, one stole a biscuit one night from the grub box, and when Merriam fired into the treetop it dropped the biscuit at his feet....

Bailey: MAMMALS AND LIFE ZONES OF OREGON

NORTHWEST SPECIES

NORTHERN FLYING SQUIRREL *Glaucomys sabrinus* 11 3/4 · 5 1/2 (300-131)

A small, nocturnal, brownish-gray squirrel with a large round head, large black eyes, and soft silky fur. Under parts ashy gray to light buffy. Prominent fur-covered membranes along sides between fore and hind feet. Gliding habit in traveling from tree to tree is characteristic. Strongly restricted to coniferous forests throughout the Northwest, excepting Vancouver Island, southeastern Oregon, and southwestern Idaho.

Northern Pocket Gopher (Naches, Washington; J.R.C.)

Northern Pocket Gopher pushing soil out of burrow (Naches, Washington; J.R.C.)

Northern Pocket Gopher mounds amid volcanic ash (12 miles east of Vantage, Washington; J.R.C.)

POCKET GOPHERS

Pocket gophers are medium-sized rodents distinguished by their externally opening fur-lined cheek pouches used for carrying food, large yellow incisors, and long-clawed front feet suitably adapted for digging. Their fur is short, their eyes are small but clearly evident, and their scantily-haired tails are relatively short. They may be separated from the moles with which they are often confused by several means. Moles' eyes are not apparent, their front feet are more spade-like, their tails are shorter, and their muzzles are less rodent-like. Pocket gophers are excellent diggers and, unlike the moles which often merely push the soil out of their way, dig true tunnels, the soil from which is removed from the burrows to the surface to form mounds or hills. Only in the Townsend's Mole do we find expertise in tunneling comparable to that of the gopher. The group of mammals treated here are active in winter and continue their burrowing, either in the soil or in the snow.

Six species of pocket gophers occur variously in the Pacific Northwest. The Southern Pocket Gopher has two small ranges in s.w. Oregon. The large Townsend's Pocket Gopher likewise occupies areas of small extent in s.e. Oregon and s. Idaho unlike the widely-occurring Northern Pocket Gopher which extends throughout the Pacific Northwest except for timbered lowland areas in s. B.C. and s. Washington and Oregon. Gopher areas in the coastal parts of Washington and Oregon contain the closely similar Mazama Pocket Gopher. The large, dark Camas Pocket Gopher exists entirely in the Willamette Valley of Oregon, while the small Idaho Pocket Gopher is found in eastern Idaho.

As is indicated above, much of the Northwest is populated by pocket gophers. Their presence is revealed by the numerous hills of excavated earth in summer and the earth cores or cables lying on the ground uncovered by melting snow in early spring. In some alpine areas, the meadows may be literally laced with these mysterious cores. They are the work of the pocket gophers which, having tunneled in the ground after burrowing in the snow during the winter, place the soil tailings in old snow tunnels. As the snow slumps and melts, these cores are slowly lowered to the earth's surface and finally liberated from their snow molds as the white stuff disappears. After a few weeks of drying out, the cores fall apart and their rope-like shape is destroyed. Pocket gophers are active throughout the winter. The author and a companion, while traveling over a snowy meadow in a snowmobile, surprised a coyote in the act of digging a gopher out of its snow burrow. The coyote fled the scene with the gopher, but left one of the rodent's legs in the dug-out burrow.

In spite of their biological interest, pocket gophers may constitute a serious menace to man's economy in gardens and agricultural fields by consuming food and piling up hills of dirt over young plants. If a few individuals are the culprits in a small garden, a few gopher traps will suffice. In large areas, however, the use of strychnine-poisoned grain or diced cubes of potatoes or carrots must be employed.

Gophers forage by underground tunneling, seeking roots, tubers, and bulbs of various plants. Most activity of the animals is spent below the surface with only brief visits above the ground, mainly for pushing out excavated soil. In its underground domain, the gopher patiently tunnels along, seeking food, extending its burrow system, well away from whatever weather may be prevailing "outside." Gophers are consistently solitary

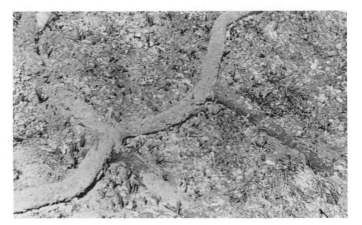

Pocket Gopher earth cables (Naches, Washington; J.R.C.)

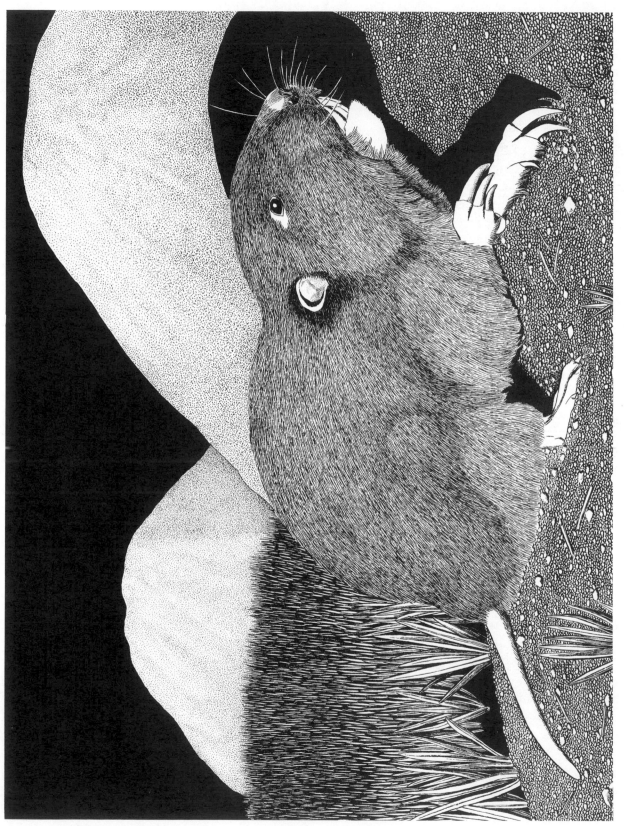

Northern Pocket Gopher

and each burrow system possesses only a single occupant which is not at all agreeable to the approach of other gophers. This antagonism is relaxed during the breeding season in meetings of opposite sexes. After a gestation period of shortly less than three weeks, the five or six young are born. The pocket gopher does not hibernate, but burrows through the snow, if present, in its search for food.

No treatment of Pacific Northwest gophers would be complete without mention of the Mima Mounds on Mima Prairie south of Olympia. Literally immense gopher hills, these are an amazing sight and should be watched for by anyone driving through the area. The subject of long and continuous controversy, Victor B. Scheffer and Walter W. Dalquest originally suggested the origin of the mounds by pocket gophers. Great were the expostulations of the geologists that followed. One of the latter group's hypotheses has it that these mounds are the result of permafrost activity. The last glacial period ended some 10,000 years ago and it is difficult to imagine how permafrost boils could remain un-eroded that long, unless, of course, permafrost heaving still exists in the area!
Larrison: MAMMALS OF THE NORTHWEST

NORTHWEST SPECIES

NORTHERN POCKET GOPHER *Thomomys talpoides* 7 7/8 · 2 3/8 (200-60)
A small to medium-sized pocket gopher varying from yellowish brown to dark brownish. Nose and ear patches are blackish. Open areas, subalpine parks, open woods, pastures, etc. in eastern Washington, east and central Oregon, Idaho, and southeastern and southcentral British Columbia.

IDAHO POCKET GOPHER *Thomomys idahoensis* 6 5/8 · 1 7/8 (170-48)
A small yellowish or buffy pocket gopher with whitish feet. Open areas in eastcentral and southeastern Idaho.

MAZAMA POCKET GOPHER *Thomomys mazama* 8 1/3 · 2 2/3 (208-66)
Very similar externally to the Northern Pocket Gopher. Best separated from that species by range for the purposes of this book. Open prairies and subalpine meadows in western Oregon [including the Cascades] and western Washington.

CAMAS POCKET GOPHER *Thomomys bulbivorus* 11 3/4 · 3 1/2 (300-90)
A very large dark brown or blackish pocket gopher. Open habitats in the Willamette Valley of Oregon.

VALLEY POCKET GOPHER *Thomomys bottae* 9 3/8 · 3 (240-78)
A medium-sized pocket gopher with reddish-brown upper parts and light buffy (tinged with rusty) under parts. Feet, cheeks, and chin are white. Open areas in southwestern Oregon.

TOWNSEND'S POCKET GOPHER *Thomomys townsendi* 11 · 7 1/8 (280-80)
A large, buffy, grayish, brownish, or blackish pocket gopher. Agricultural areas in southeastern Oregon and southern Idaho.

Great Basin Pocket Mouse

POCKET MICE

The rodent family Heteromyidae to which the pocket mice and the two groups that follow belong is a unique and interesting one. For several reasons. They have externally-opening fur-lined cheek pouches in which they can transport seeds and bits of vegetation which they have gathered on the surface of the ground to their subsurface burrows and caches. As there is a tendency in this family for bipedal or saltatorial locomotion — that is, hopping on the hind legs — the posterior pair of limbs is well developed and larger and longer than the anterior ones. Because of the common use of this mode of progression, these mammals must frequent open habitats where the vegetation is sparse and not impeding their rapid sallies over the ground. Members of the group also show an interesting proclivity of preferring certain types of soil surface or restriction to soils of particular colors — thus a number of species in this group called "soil color" forms or races. A good example in the Pacific Northwest region would be the blackish pocket mice of the lava beds of the Craters of the Moon area of southern Idaho.

Smallest of the pocket mice and the smallest mouse in the Northwest is the Little Pocket Mouse. Larrison first discovered this species as a part of the Idaho mammal fauna many years ago in an interesting way. E. Raymond Hall in his monumental account of the mammals of Nevada listed them as a part of that state's fauna and gave some locality records not far below the Idaho line. At the time, Larrison was doing field work in the Raft River Valley of extreme southern Idaho. Hall noted in his book that these mice were particularly to be found on alluvial fans, the surface of which was covered with pea-sized gravel from sheet washing. Larrison could see a number of these fans from the motel windows where he was staying and had noted their gravel-covered surface on a reconnaissance hike. Immediately sacking up a batch of museum special traps, he made for the nearest fan and laid out several lines. The next morning, he was rewarded with a new state record.

Great Basin Pocket Mouse (dunes north of Pasco, Washington; J.R.C.)

The larger Great Basin Pocket Mouse is much more widely distributed, occurring in desert and semi-desert areas throughout the interior of the region. It exists in a number of varieties from the pale-colored *clarus* to the blackish *idahoensis* mentioned above in the Craters of the Moon.

Pocket mice are attractive little rodents with interesting habits and structure and soft silky fur. How different from the common House Mouse of dirty appearance and distasteful habits.

NORTHWEST SPECIES

GREAT BASIN POCKET MOUSE *Perognathus parvus* 7 1/8 - 3 1/2 (180-90)
Medium-sized pocket mouse (silky fur, large hind legs, external cheek pouches), light to dark gray or blackish above and white to buffy below. Sagebrush, rabbitbrush, and adjacent grainfields in arid parts of eastern Washington and eastern Oregon, as well as southern Idaho and southcentral British Columbia.

LITTLE POCKET MOUSE *Perognathus longimembris* 5 1/8 - 2 3/4 (130-71)
A tiny mouse, buffy gray above with a grizzling of blackish hairs and whitish to pale buffy below. Hind legs longer than fore legs. Externally opening fur-lined cheek pouches identify it as a heteromyid. Southeastern Oregon and the Raft River Valley of Idaho, in sagebrush and shadscale.

Dark Kangaroo Mouse

Habitat of the Dark Kangaroo Mouse (Owyhee desert near Oreana, Idaho; E.J.L.)

KANGAROO MICE

Like their relatives, the kangaroo rats and pocket mice, these quaint little gnomes are desert dwellers, lovers of sandy or mellow soil among the sagebrush and are able to live where there is little rain or long periods of drought. They are nocturnal burrowers, sleeping underground during the day and rarely seen except when taken in traps at night. The little paired tracks of the two hind feet, too large for pocket mice and too small for kangaroo rats, are easily recognized in the dusty trails, but the closed burrows, well hidden under the sagebrush, are not easily found. Like many other small animals they will follow a long mark made with the foot in the soft soil and may be caught in traps set delicately across these artificial trails and baited with rolled oats.

They run in short hops on the two hind feet, rarely leaving a print of the little hands, which are generally folded on the breast and used mostly for feeding, digging, and all the general purposes of hands rather than feet. Their speed is so great that when frightened they disappear like a flash of light over the sandy soil of their own color. In captivity, if quietly handled, they are gentle and unafraid. They are closely like the kangaroo rats in disposition and habits.

Living in the dry, hot sandy desert they might be supposed to be very thirsty animals, but as they are out only at night when the air close to the ground is moist and cool, and spend the daytime in closed burrows a foot below the surface in a cool, moist atmosphere, they probably do not require a great amount of water and the little they need can be readily secured at any time from their food.

It would be difficult to accord any commercial or economic value to these dainty little denizens of the desert nor can any serious sins of omission or commission be laid to them. Still they have a value sufficient to warrant many in making a long journey in the desert to gain a few specimens of a unique type and to learn a little of the causes that have guided its development along lines different from all other forms of life. As the writer looks back more than 45 years to the capture of the type of this genus and the first thrill of realizing its remarkable characters, so different from even its nearest relatives and opening up a whole new field of possibilities for the multiform kinds of desert life, it is no wonder that the hardships of bitter winter and scorching summer camps should have vanished before the fascination of this first-hand study of desert life. With all our intelligence and versatility of adaptation we are still far behind such animals in the perfection of physical mechanisms for our needs, and we can surely learn humility if not wisdom from many of our inferior mammalian brothers.

Bailey: MAMMALS AND LIFE ZONES
OF OREGON

NORTHWEST SPECIES

DARK KANGAROO MOUSE *Microdipodops megacephalus* 6 1/4 - 3 9/16 (159-90)
A small mouse-sized kangaroo-like rodent with typical fur-lined cheek pouches of the heteromyids, large hind feet, small fore feet, and a closely-haired tail that is thick in the middle and tapering to a point at the tip. Buffy gray above, whitish to light buffy below. Diminutive size and thickened tail distinctive. Sandy soil in desert areas in widely scattered localities in southeastern Oregon and southwestern Idaho.

Ord's Kangaroo Rat

KANGAROO RATS

As mentioned previously, these are members of the heteromyid family and exhibit best the leaping habits of the group. Large size, fur-lined externally-opening cheek pouches, and large hind feet complete the identification of the kangaroo rats. As with the pocket mice, many species of this genus (*Dipodomys*) show interesting specific preferences for soil and terrain types. Two examples of Northwest "K-rats" will merit mention.

The Ord's Kangaroo Rat reflects its relatively great tolerance of desert and semi-desert conditions in its large geographic range, the most extensive of any of the genus. In the Northwest, it occurs widely in the Great Basin and related areas, being most numerous in sandy weedy places and in the sagebrush generally. It appears not only to occur in, but to seek out habitats with a varied vegetation. This phenomenon is reflected in its breadth of food habits, as well. The Chisel-toothed Kangaroo Rat, in contrast, shows a preference for chenopods and light loessial or ashy soils. In the Great Basin, we have found them most readily in stands of shadscale, salt sage, or winterfat, especially in very light soils. Here, their low mounds and many runways are evident on even casual inspection.

Burrow and trails of the Ord's Kangaroo Rat (Cassia Co., Idaho; E.J.L.)

69

NORTHWEST SPECIES

ORD'S KANGAROO RAT *Dipodomys ordi* 9 3/4 · 5 1/2 (250·140)
Body dark tannish above, white below with long tail and large hind and small fore feet. Soles of feet and linings of cheek pouches white. Lower incisors taper to sharp points. Sandy dusty sagebrush and weedy areas in southcentral Washington, eastern Oregon, and southern Idaho.

CHISEL-TOOTHED KANGAROO RAT *Dipodomys microps* 10 5/8 · 6 3/8 (270·160)
Similar to the Ord's K-rat but darker, with sooty fur on the soles of the feet and linings of the cheek pouches. Lower incisors broad and chisel-shaped and not tapering to points. Chenopod vegetation in ashy soils in southeastern Oregon and southwestern and central southern Idaho. The chisel-like lower incisors are used in scraping off the high salt containing skin of the chenopods on which it feeds.

HEERMANN'S KANGAROO RAT *Dipodomys heermanni* 12 1/4 · 7 3/16 (312·184)
Larger than the above two rats and darker, especially on the face, head, and back. Open habitats in Klamath and Brownsboro area in southwestern Oregon.

Ord's Kangaroo Rat (dunes north of Pasco, Washington; J.R.C.)

Indian Rice Grass, Tall Green Rabbit Brush, and Spiny Hopsage of Ord's Kangaroo Rat habitat (dunes north of Pasco, Washington; J.R.C.)

Mound and burrows of the Chisel-toothed Kangaroo Rat (Owyhee Desert, Idaho; E.J.L.)

BEAVERS

The beaver of this country is large and fat; the flesh is very palatable, and at our table was a real luxury. On the 7th of January, 1806, our hunter (Drewyer) found a beaver in his traps, of which he made a bait for taking others. This bait will entice the beaver to the trap from as far as he can smell it, which may be fairly stated to be at the distance of a mile, as their sense of smelling is very acute. To prepare beaver bait, the castor or bark-stone is first gently pressed from the bladder-like bag which contains it, into a phial of four ounces, with a large mouth. Five or six of these stones are thus taken, to which must be added a nutmeg, 12 or 15 cloves, and 30 grains of cinnamon, finely pulverized and stirred together, with as much ardent spirits added to the composition as will reduce the whole to the consistency of mustard. This must be carefully corked, as it soon loses its efficacy if exposed to open air. The scent becomes stronger in four or five days after preparation, and provided proper precaution is exercised, will provide its efficacy for months. Any strong aromatic spices will answer, their sole virtue being to give variety and pungency to the scent of the bark-stone. The male beaver has six stones, two of which contain a substance much like finely pulverized bark, of a pale tan color, in smell resembling tanner's ooze; these are called bark-stones, or castors. Two others, which like the bark-stones resemble small bladders, contain pure oil of a rank smell, and are called the oil-stones; the other two are the testicles. The bark-stones are two inches in length; the other are somewhat smaller, of an oval form, and lie in a bunch together, between the skin and the root of the tail, with which they are closely connected and seem to communicate. The female brings forth once in a year only, and has sometimes two and sometimes four at a birth, which usually happens in the latter end of May and the beginning of June; at this time, she is said to drive from the lodge the male, which would otherwise destroy the young ....

.... we also procured three beavers, which are quite gentle, they have not been hunted, though when the hunters are in pursuit they never leave their huts during the day. This animal we esteem a great delicacy, particularly the tail, which when boiled resembles in flavor the fleshy tongues and sounds of the codfish, and is generally so large as to afford a plentiful meal for two men....

We saw many otter and beaver today. The latter seem to contribute very much to the number of islands and the widening of the river. They begin by damming up the small channels of about 20 yards between the islands; this obliges the river to seek another outlet, and as soon as this is effected the channel stopped by the beaver

Swimming Beaver (at Northwest Trek; J.R.C.)

Beaver skeletons at a skinning site used by Peter Skene Ogden's Hudson Bay trapping brigade in 1826 (Owyhee Co., Idaho; E.J.L.)

American Beaver

becomes filled with mud and sand. The industrious animal is then driven to another channel, which soon shares the same fate, till the river spreads on all sides and cuts the projecting points of the land into islands....

Two hunters were dispatched early in the morning, but they returned without killing anything, and the only game we procured was a beaver caught last night in a trap, which he carried off two miles before he was found. The fur of this animal is as good as any we have seen, nor does it, in fact, appear to be ever out of season on the upper branches of the Missouri. This beaver, with several dozen fine trout, gave us a plentiful subsistence for the day....

Lewis and Clark: COUES' EDITION OF THE JOURNALS

The above passages are quoted from the journals of Lewis and Clark written on their memorable journey of exploration to the Pacific Northwest in 1804-1806. Traveling much of the time by canoe or keelboat, they had ample opportunity to see and study this interesting rodent.

The coming into fashion of the beaver felt hat a dozen or so years after the expedition, put a premium on the hides of the beaver and it became the object of a romantic, though brief, trapping industry. The fearless mountain man, as he was styled, braved winter blizzard, summer sun, and hostile Indians to secure the "plews" of this animal, many of which were shipped to Europe to furnish the felt from which fashionable top hats were made. A great service rendered by these hardy men was the exploration of the mountainous West, a job that perhaps would have been performed successfully only by such persons.

NORTHWEST SPECIES

BEAVER *Castor canadensis* 39 1/2 · 17 3/4 (1,000-450)
A large dark brown rodent with a large blunt head and a distinctive, flattened, scale-covered tail. Impossible to mistake for any other animal. Some individuals may weigh as much as 30 to 60 pounds. Occurs in a variety of lakes, ponds (often of their own making), and streams and rivers throughout the Northwest.

Beaver lodge in lake (Pend Oreille Co., Washington; E.J.L.)

Beaver dam on backwater of the Yakima River (near Union Gap, Washington; J.R.C.)

Beaver channel in the ice of a lake, kept open as long as possible (Pend Oreille Co.; E.J.L.)

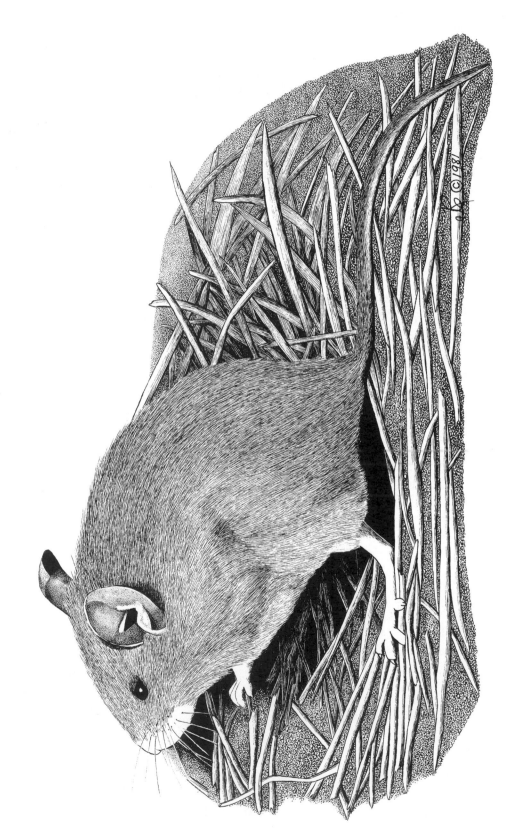

Western Harvest Mouse

HARVEST MICE

The American harvest mice (genus *Reithrodontomys)* are small brownish mice looking very much like House Mice. The upper incisors of the harvest mice, however, are grooved, unlike the incisors of the House Mice. The five species of *Reithrodontomys* pretty well cover the United States with the exception of the northeastern part. Only one form, the Western Harvest Mouse, is to be found in the Pacific Northwest. This is an animal of the dry interior areas in our region and even at that its distribution is spotty, as it seems to prefer dense vegetation, such as weedy patches, giant wild rye, Russian thistle, usually, but not always near water. We have found that wild rye patches near desert streams are particularly good places for populations of this mouse.

NORTHWEST SPECIES

WESTERN HARVEST MOUSE *Reithrodontomys megalotis* 5 1/2 - 2 11/16 (141-69)
A small mouse, brownish above and buffy gray below, with

long bicolored tail, tannish hairs inside the ears, and grooved upper incisors. Dense grass and cattails in the dry lowland interior of the Northwest.

Harvest Mouse (mouth of Tieton River, Yakima Co., Washington; J.R.C.)

Greasewood, Giant Wild Rye, and Salt Grass *(Distichlis stricta),* a Harvest Mouse habitat (J.R.C.)

Giant Wild Rye *(Elymus cinereus),* a very excellent Harvest Mouse habitat (J.R.C.)

Common Deer Mouse

DEER MICE

Of the approximately 16 species of mice of the genus *Peromyscus* in North America, five are to be found in the Pacific Northwest. One of these, the Common Deer Mouse (*Peromyscus maniculatus*), occurs throughout almost all of North America with the exception of the extreme Arctic regions. Of Northwest deer mice, this species is also the most widely distributed and numerous. It is to be found in most brushy, wooded, or rocky habitats, except those small areas occupied by the other four species (see range summaries in species accounts).

The mice in this genus are usually the most abundant mammals in the areas they inhabit and as such constitute an important part of the food base for many small and medium-sized predators. Basically brush mice, trees are not necessary, as witnessed by the abundance of deer mice in the sagebrush plains. In the grainfields of the Palouse country of eastern Washington, they are common, possibly being attracted by the plentiful supply of waste grain seeds, particularly at harvest time.

NORTHWEST SPECIES

COMMON DEER MOUSE *Peromyscus maniculatus* 7 - 2 15/16 (180-74)
Medium-sized, long-eared, long-tailed mouse, brownish above and whitish below. Tail strongly bicolored. Abundant throughout the Northwest with exception of the Washington Cascades, Olympic Peninsula, and Coast Range of British Columbia. In practically all habitats.

MOUNTAIN DEER MOUSE *Peromyscus oreas* 7 7/8 - 4 5/16 (202-110)
Similar to Common Deer Mouse but much larger. Montane forests of the Cascades and Olympics of Washington and the Coast Range of British Columbia; also irregularly in the lowlands of southwestern Washington.

SITKA DEER MOUSE *Peromyscus sitkensis* 8 9/16 - 4 1/16 (219-104)
A large dark-colored deer mouse. Occurs on certain islands in the Alaska Panhandle Archipelago.

CANYON MOUSE *Peromyscus crinitus* 7 1/4 - 3 3/4 (185-96)
Medium-sized dark-buffy mouse with a long tail and white belly. Occurs in rockslides and along cliffs in deep canyons in the dry country of the interior of eastern Oregon and southern Idaho.

PINYON MOUSE *Peromyscus truei* 7 1/4 - 3 9/16 (185-91)
Very similar to the Common Deer Mouse but with much larger ears (inch or more in length). In scattered areas near juniper in southern Idaho and southern and westcentral Oregon.

Tracks of a Common Deer Mouse in the snow (Pend Oreille Co., Washington; E.J.L.)

Juniper woodland edge habitat of the Pinyon Deer Mouse (Cassia Co., Idaho; E.J.L.)

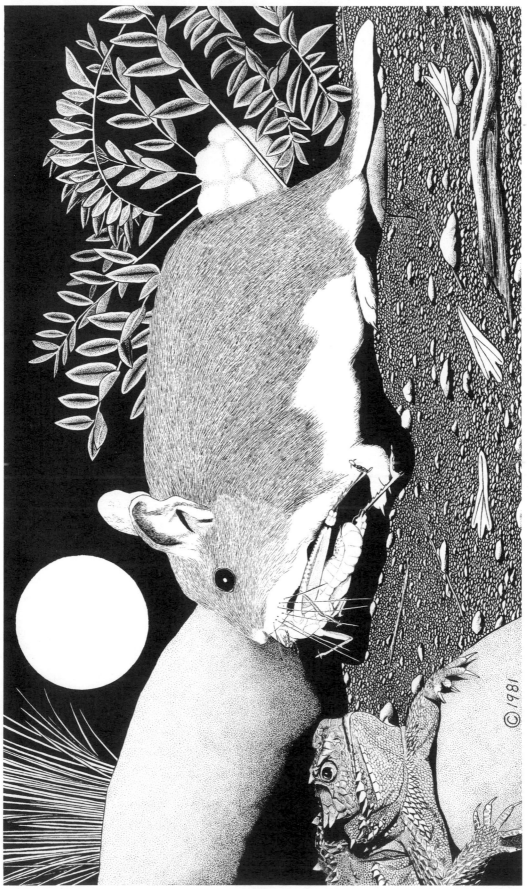

Northern Grasshopper Mouse

GRASSHOPPER MICE

These insectivorous and carnivorous little rodents have many of the habits of the weasel family. They are hunters, wanderers, freebooters, apparently never common, and without permanent homes of their own. They are generally caught in traps set for other animals at any kind of burrow or in trails or long marks made by running the heel or toe along the surface of the ground to be followed by inquisitive animals. They evidently frequent and probably appropriate the burrows of other small rodents, driving out or eating the owners at will. Their large front feet and claws suggest digging powers, but the writer has never found burrows that could be attributed to them and suspects that the claws are weapons rather than tools. They are much used in catching and holding their prey and also used in fighting and for defensive purposes.

In many years of trapping these animals for specimens about all that could be learned of their habits was from the contents of the stomachs of those caught and from the many species of other small animals eaten by them when caught in traps. From captive individuals, however, much concerning their habits and natures has been learned. One taken on the south side of Malheur Lake on August 31, 1920, was kept alive for nearly 3 years. He was not afraid from the first but was not so gentle and tame as others kept in captivity. He resented being handled and would bark and nip one's fingers, and if bothered too much, would on rare occasions actually bite. He was exceedingly quick and nimble and not easily caught in the hands, even in his cage.

While mainly nocturnal, he could see well in any light and came out of his nest box at any time when hungry, or if he heard the footfall of an insect or smelled a mouse of some other species.

He was a keen hunter and often searched his cage for any grasshopper, cricket, beetle, or scorpion that might be available. He would pounce on them and kill them, even though he did not eat them at the time. A live mouse in his cage was hunted down and cornered, if it could not be cap-

A sagebrush plain in the Owyhee Desert of Idaho, a good habitat for the Grasshopper Mouse (E.J.L.)

tured in the open. He would persistently follow its trail, creeping up in the grass, eager, alert, tail twitching, until he could pounce upon it. If he got a good hold, the struggle was short, and the mouse quickly dropped, limp and helpless, as his long sharp lower incisors penetrated its brain near one ear. If the mouse was of his own size and caught by the back end, there was a rough-and-tumble mix-up. The victim might be allowed to escape in order that a better hold might be obtained next time, but the pursuer was persistent and only awaited his chance. White-footed and meadow mice of his own size were regularly killed and eaten. In one case a white-footed mouse was not killed, and two mornings later it was sleeping with him in a better nest than he usually made for himself. For a couple of weeks he lived with the white-footed mouse on friendly terms, possibly awaiting for a scarcity of food, or he may have been lonesome or cold, or needed a good nest builder as assistant. The white-footed mouse was then returned to his home in the sagebrush and *Onychomys* accompanied his captors on a long journey....

Bailey: MAMMALS AND LIFE ZONES OF OREGON

NORTHWEST SPECIES

NORTHERN GRASSHOPPER MOUSE *Onychomys leucogaster* 5 3/16 · 1 9/16 (138-40)
A stocky medium-sized mouse, grayish above and white below with a very short (1 1/2 inch) tail. Sagebrush areas of eastern Washington and Oregon and southern Idaho.

An old log cabin in Idaho; another good habitat for the "pack rat" (E.J.L.)

Basaltic cliffs and talus in the Grand Coulee, Washington; prime habitat of the Bushy-tailed Wood Rat (J.R.C.)

A rockslide with very large boulders is a likely habitat for the Bushy-tailed Wood Rat (E.J.L.)

WOOD RATS

Our wood rats are probably best known for some three features, their strong musky odors, their immense nests and stick piles, and their thieving behavior which has dubbed them with their better known name of "pack rats".

Occurring widely in the forested areas of the Pacific Northwest is the large Bushy-tailed Wood Rat which may, in the authors' experience, reach a pound in weight and 18 inches in total length. Our experiences with these animals, especially their thieving proclivities, would fill a volume this size. Larrison, as a young child, first encountered them when one night they took off, bean by bean, the family's supply of lima beans when the Larrisons were camped at the old Soda Springs resort on Ahtanum Creek southwest of Yakima. Being the possessor of false teeth and eye-glasses, Larrison now has to make sure that these items are securely cached when he tents out!

We have found that wood rats have a habit of seeking inside quarters in late August or early September, probably in preparation for winter. Forest cabins and wilderness farm houses have to be carefully closed up or one of these mammals will settle down with you. Some of our readers have undoubtedly experienced the mess that a pack rat can make of a cabin. What food is not eaten will be fouled with urine and feces. Mattresses and sleeping bags will be torn open and a strong odor imparted to the rooms.

Larrison once had an amusing experience with a large pack rat and its unwilling hosts. He and a field assistant were doing collecting in the Raft River Valley of Idaho and making our base at the little town of Malta. We took our meals at Joe Willett's Valley Cafe. One evening, Joe told us that he had a very big pack rat in his house next to the restaurant and would we remove it for him. We didn't get around to doing the job the next day and at dinner time that night we were reminded of

Nest of the Desert Wood Rat (Cassia Co., Idaho; E.J.L.)

Bushy-tailed Wood Rat

our job and that the rat had now set up housekeeping in the bathroom and had stolen the soap. Delays of one kind or another still prevented us from trapping for the rat and a couple of evenings later, the proprietor of the cafe informed us that "the rat was as big as a dog, that they were afraid to enter the room, that it has stolen the bathtub stopper, and that if we planned on taking further meals at his establishment, we had better get busy and remove the rat — pronto!" So, we immediately installed some rat traps in the Willett bathroom. The next morning, we found that they had all been sprung, but were empty. After experiencing this happening another night, we laid eight rat traps together, their "business ends" touching and the following morning an immense 18-inch Bushy-tailed Wood Rat was caught, but it had taken several traps to hold and kill it. The specimen now reposes in the University of Idaho mammal collection — and we continued to eat at Joe Willett's cafe.

NORTHWEST SPECIES

DESERT WOOD RAT *Neotoma lepida* 11 - 4 5/8 (280-118)
Small grayish to buffy-gray wood rat with a closely furred (not bushy) tail. Sagebrush and northern shrub desert areas in southeastern Oregon and southern Idaho. Particularly to be found in hop sage tracts.

DUSKY-FOOTED WOOD RAT *Neotoma fuscipes* 18 5/8 - 8 7/16 (445-216)
Large wood rat, dark brown above and buffy to reddish buffy below, and with dusky feet (but with white toes). Tail not bushy. Brushy and open woods in western Oregon.

BUSHY-TAILED WOOD RAT *Neotoma cinerea* 15 3/4 - 6 7/8 (400-175)
Medium-sized to large wood rat, grayish brown above and white below with white feet and a bushy squirrel-like tail. Rocky areas and abandoned buildings and mines in forested areas, as well as open desert regions, throughout the Northwest.

Montane Meadow Mouse

©1981

84

VOLES

The first week in July at Indian Henrys, with 4 feet of snow on the ground, the animals [water voles] were occasionally noted during the middle of the day, sitting about the entrances of their snow tunnels like little rabbits, showing little fear of the intruder. With care one could approach to within a few feet of them. Later in the summer they were much shyer and almost never seen in a quiet pose. At Reflection Lake one was watched beneath a mountain ash bush for nearly two minutes. It moved about quickly, stopping at short intervals and blinking in the sunlight. The animal gives one an impression of dumpiness or sluggishness (one was caught by Shaw in his hands), though usually it runs like other meadow mice or red-backed mice, making a fairly rapid non-stop run until safe within its burrow....

In addition to its daytime activities, the large-footed meadow mouse [water vole] is one of the most industrious of night workers as was conclusively demonstrated one evening at St. Andrews Park. Our camp bed having been made on a thick cushion of heather, we retired as usual, when shortly we noticed a crunching or scratching sound, apparently immediately beneath our heads. Then we heard similar sounds under the foot of the bed. This amused and interested us for a short time, but presently it became somewhat monotonous. Repeated kicks, accompanied finally by vocal imprecations, did not avail to silence the energetic workers. We had placed our bed over a network of meadow-mouse runways; and apparently the animals were busy, night and day, in cutting the blueberry brush (*Vaccinium deliciosum*) and other accessible vegetation. Fortunately, they confined their activities strictly to the native plants and did not touch any of our camp equipment....

In summer the heather vole (*Phenacomys intermedius*) is found in the shelter of the heathers (*Phyllodoce empetriformis* and *Cassiope mertensiana*) frequently among the snow patches near the glaciers. It occurs also in log-tangled grassy burns at a lower elevation, as well as on dry hillslopes in shrubbery made up chiefly of huckleberry, *(Luetkea pectinata)* and avalanche lily *(Erythronium montanum)*. Occasionally it penetrates the heavily timbered Canadian Zone, for one was secured at Mountain Meadows (4,000 feet) on a mossy rock at the creek margin near a waterfall. At the other extreme it ranges into the Arctic-Alpine Zone, reaching at least 2,000 feet above timber line, several nests being seen on the slopes of Mount Ruth (altitude about 8,500 feet). During the winter the lemmings from the higher slopes probably descend to the border of the open park country, a habitat then shared with the large-footed meadow mouse.

The habits of the lemming mouse are, however, quite different from those of its large rodent relative and the winter work of each is distinct even when in the same territory. Areas occupied by the large-footed meadow mouse are usually riddled with holes, littered with remains of vegetation, and piled with earthen mounds. The lemming mouse, on the other hand, leaves scarce a trace of its occupation, save for the conspicuous and characteristic under-snow nests....

With its graceful movements and attractive though modest coloration, the red-backed mouse is always an interesting park resident. If one will walk out into the thick timber near Longmire Springs and watch quietly for some minutes he is almost sure to catch sight of one. Maybe a streak and a shadow is all he will see, but often the mouse will proceed with deliberation sufficient to afford an adequate view. Perhaps the animal will run nimbly to the top of a stump and then vanish from sight in a hole; or it may disappear in an old root excavation; or it may run along or under a huge log; or may even climb a spruce or fir, though it rarely gets so far as 15 feet from the ground....

Ordinarily the red-back prefers the root-entangled, moss protected forest floor in the deepest woods; but individuals are frequently trapped along creek banks, in the tall grass of mountain parks, in thick meadow vegetation such as false hellebore *(Veratrum)* in dry places beneath huckleberry or *Menziesia* brush, or in piles of bark fragments. Considering this variability of habitat, it is not strange that the mouse occurs from the heavily forested country near Longmire to near timber line. In fact, Doctor Merriam's party, in 1897, found it next to the large-footed meadow mouse, the most abundant timber-line mammal on the mountain.

It will be remembered that heavy snows often persist on the slopes of Mount Rainier until well into the summer. This was the case during 1919. At Indian Henrys early in July the groups of black hemlocks and alpine firs looked like dark green islands in a sea of snowy white. Several species of mice were abundant. Not infrequently red-backs were seen traversing the well-traveled runways over the bare ground or running about over the snow from their numerous tunnels beneath the white blanket to the open spaces under the trees. What highways of travel these runways were! Hundreds of furry, bright-eyed creatures, red-back mice, meadow mice, deer mice, and shrews,

in summer distributed widely over the broad acres of meadowland, were now concentrated in very narrow limits about the tree stumps; and it is quite likely that, for the time being, they were short of food and foraging space.

Taylor and Shaw: MAMMALS AND BIRDS OF MOUNT RAINIER NATIONAL PARK

NORTHWEST SPECIES

COMMON MEADOW MOUSE *Microtus agrestis* 7 · 1 3/4 (176-46)
A moderately large vole, blackish brown in color (only slightly paler below) with a very short tail. Fur is glossy. Wet boggy meadows and streamsides in British Columbia (excepting the coastal region), northcentral and northeastern Washington, and northern, central, and eastern Idaho. Formerly known as *Microtus pennsylvanicus.*

MONTANE MEADOW MOUSE *Microtus montanus* 6 1/4 · 1 1/2 (160-39)
A medium-sized vole, dark brownish above and dark grayish below with a short tail and grayish feet. Meadows, pastures, and weedy ditches in eastern Oregon and

Weedy roadside ditch habitat of the Montane Meadow Mouse, Vagrant Shrew, and Common Deer Mouse (Kamiak Butte, Washington; E.J.L.)

Washington, southcentral British Columbia, and most of Idaho. Mostly in the lowlands and foothills.

GRAY-TAILED MEADOW MOUSE *Microtus canicaudus* 6 - 1 1/3 (154-34)
A small vole with yellowish gray or brown upper parts and grayish white under parts. Tail is short and bicolored. Feet are grayish. Grassy areas and pastures in northwestern Oregon and the Vancouver area of Washington.

CALIFORNIA MEADOW MOUSE *Microtus californicus* 6 11/16 - 1 7/8 (171-49)
A medium-sized meadow mouse, brownish above and grayish below, with a bicolored tail. Mostly in meadows in southwestern Oregon.

TOWNSEND'S MEADOW MOUSE *Microtus townsendi* 9 - 2 2/3 (225-66)
A large meadow mouse with glossy dark-brownish upper parts, brownish or reddish sides, and dark grayish under parts. Tail is long and not bicolored. Lowland swamps and marshes, as well as subalpine meadows in the Olympics and on Vancouver Island. Western Washington and Oregon

and extreme southwestern British Columbia mainland, as well as Vancouver Island.

TUNDRA MEADOW MOUSE *Microtus oeconomus* 6 13/16 - 1 15/16 (174-50)
A medium-sized meadow mouse with brownish upper parts, buffy gray under parts, and yellowish-brown sides. Feet are grayish. Occurs in tundra in the extreme northwest tip of British Columbia.

Marshy habitat of the Common Meadow Mouse (Pend Oreille Co., Washington; E.J.L.)

Winter burrows of the Montane Meadow Mouse, chewed through the grass mat under the snow (Larrison's front yard, Moscow, Idaho; E.J.L.)

Lowland wooded habitat of the Oregon Meadow Mouse (Stillaguamish River, Washington; E.J.L.)

87

Streamside habitat of the Water Vole in dense grass on steep banks along a creek. Note the traps nested in runways (Kootenay Lake, British Columbia; E.J.L.)

LONG-TAILED MEADOW MOUSE *Microtus longicaudus* 7 1/4 · 2 7/16 (183-63)
A moderately large long-tailed meadow mouse with brownish or grayish-brown upper parts and grayish sides and under parts. Occurs in moist places, as well as relatively dry tall grass patches, throughout much of the Northwest, excluding northeastern British Columbia, Vancouver Island, and western Oregon. Note: Relative sizes of bodies and tails, as well as coloration and glossiness or dullness of fur, are important clues to the superficial identification of voles.

OREGON MEADOW MOUSE; CREEPING MEADOW MOUSE *Microtus oregoni* 5 1/4 · 1 3/5 (140-42)
A small completely dark brown meadow mouse with very short tail and ears. Occurs in wet (also dry) meadows and damp woods from lowlands to subalpine areas in western Washington and Oregon and extreme southwestern British Columbia. More commonly found in woodlands than any other meadow mouse.

SINGING MEADOW MOUSE *Microtus miurus* 5 15/16 · 1 3/16 (152-30)
A medium-sized, short-tailed mouse, brownish above and slightly paler below. Tail bicolored and ear spots buffy. Alpine areas of extreme northwestern British Columbia.

TUNDRA RED-BACKED MOUSE *Clethrionomys rutilus* 5 11/16 · 1 9/16 (146-41)
A small, slender, brightly-colored mouse with a bright red back, buffy belly and a short bicolored tail. Brush, open taiga forests, and tundra in northwestern British Columbia.

GAPPER'S RED-BACKED MOUSE *Clethrionomys gapperi* 5 1/2 · 1 1/2 (140-38)
A small grayish-brown mouse with a reddish back. Under parts and feet buffy white. Tail bicolored. Coniferous forests of the Northwest, except northwestern British Columbia, western Washington and Oregon, and southwestern Idaho.

WESTERN RED-BACKED MOUSE *Clethrionomys occidentalis* 6 1/16 · 2 1/16 (155-53)
Similar to the Gapper's Red-backed Mouse but larger, darker, and less reddish. Lowland coniferous forests of western Oregon and Washington and extreme southwestern British Columbia, excluding the Cascades but including the Olympics.

HEATHER MOUSE *Phenacomys intermedius* 6 · 1 3/8 (152-34)
A medium-sized vole, ashy gray to brownish above and grayish white below. Tail sharply bicolored. Fur is thick and woolly. Occurs in a variety of heather, brush, and rocky

Rock and heather habitat of the Heather Mouse (Mt. Pilchuck, Washington; E.J.L.)

Gapper's Red-backed Mouse (Mt. Shuksan, Washington; J.R.C.)

Bluebunch Wheatgrass, habitat of the Sagebrush Vole (Horse Heaven Hills, Washington; J.R.C.)

grass habitats in the mountains and foothills throughout the Northwest except southeastern Oregon and southwestern Idaho.

WHITE-FOOTED VOLE *Phenacomys (=Arborimus?) albipes* 6 11/16 - 2 7/16 (171-63)
A medium-sized mouse, brownish above and grayish below with a sharply bicolored tail and white feet. Humid coniferous forests in western Oregon. (Note: The genus *Phenacomys* needs more study as certain specimens from the Northwest do not at all resemble the described forms.)

RED TREE MOUSE *Arborimus longicaudus* 7 1/8 - 2 7/8 (182-73)
A large bright reddish mouse with whitish under parts and a long blackish tail. Coniferous forests of the lowlands and foothills in western Oregon. Prefers Douglas fir trees where it lives in the crowns and branches. Less commonly found in spruce and grand fir. Unique among North American voles. The "Dusky Tree Mouse" (*A.l. silvicola*) of northwestern Oregon may be a separate species.

RICHARDSON'S WATER VOLE *Arvicola richardsoni* 8 - 2 3/4 (220-70)
A very large vole, the largest mouse in North America, dark brown above and grayish below. Fur is dull in quality. Stiffened hairs on edges of hind feet. Occurs in immediate vicinity of mountain streams in the Cascades and Rocky Mountains of the Northwest.

SAGEBRUSH VOLE *Lagurus curtatus* 4 1/8 - 3/4 (105-20)
A small light-gray or buffy-gray vole with a very short tail. The soles of the hind feet are densely furred. To be found in grassy sagebrush and bunchgrass on elevated plateaus and foothills slopes in desert areas in eastern Washington and Oregon and southern Idaho.

BROWN LEMMING *Lemmus sibiricus* 5 7/8 - 13/16 (151-21)
A chunky, large-headed, long-haired mouse with chestnut-brown upper parts, buffy-gray under parts, and a very short tail. Fur is long and lax in texture. Occurs in tundra habitats, wet meadows, and rockslides in the mountains of northern and central British Columbia.

NORTHERN BOG LEMMING *Synaptomys borealis* 4 3/4 - 1 (122-25)
A medium-sized vole with grayish-brown upper parts, grayish under parts, short tail, and long woolly fur. There are weak longitudinal grooves near the outer edges of the anterior faces of the upper incisors between the white and yellow tooth surfaces, a condition not found in any of the other Northwest voles. Occurs along boggy stream sides and in moist grassy meadows in British Columbia (excluding Vancouver Island) south to northern and northeastern Washington and northern Idaho. A pale variety occurs on sagebrush slopes in the southern Okanagan Valley of British Columbia.

MUSKRATS

Muskrats are mainly aquatic in habits, swimming and diving with great skill, getting most of their food from under water or along shores, building houses surrounded by water, or living in bank burrows opening into the water. They are famous builders, constructing conical or dome-shaped houses of plant stems, roots, sods, and mud rising usually 3 or 4 and sometimes 5 feet above the surface of the water, with broad bases resting on the bottom of shallow lakes or ponds. A single room occupies the center of the house just above the water level with usually 2 or 3 doorways opening downward through the water and out under the house into the lake or pond. The heavy walls, often a foot thick, keep out the winter cold and many of their enemies, and the room within often accommodates a whole family of 6 or 8 animals in the moist bed of water plants close to the water level. Even in the coldest weather the inside of the house is kept warm and the water is prevented from freezing by the body warmth of the muskrats, while the porous walls admit sufficient ventilation to afford them healthy existence. In case of danger or alarm the muskrats dive quickly through the water holes and swim long distances under the water before coming to the surface, or swim under the winter ice to other houses or to bank burrows.

In deep streams or lakes the muskrats usually live in bank burrows, or tunnels leading from well under water back into the banks and upward until a nest chamber is formed above the water level. In high banks these bank dens are usually well hidden and even safer from enemies than are the house nests, and in many places both bank dens and houses are used by the same animals. There is evidently much visiting back and forth among the houses and dens, but to what extent the sociability reaches beyond the family circle is not known.

The food of muskrats consists principally of roots, tubers, bulbs, and the tender basal portion of tules, sedges, cattails, grasses, and other marsh plants. The long rhizomes of cattails, rich in starch and gluten, furnish much food, while the blanched tender basal portion of the stems of both cattails and tules are extensively eaten. Waterlily roots and leaves are a favorite food. The tender young shoots of grasses, sedges, wildrice, and numerous other green plants are eaten, while clover and alfalfa are always acceptable food. Rolled oats are eagerly eaten as are carrots and many cultivated crops, but in wild lands, grains and seeds, except wildrice, are not often obtained. Small turtles, muscles, and crawfish are sometimes eaten, but there is no evidence that fish are ever captured for food.

Bailey: MAMMALS AND LIFE ZONES OF OREGON

NORTHWEST SPECIES

MUSKRAT *Ondatra zibethicus* 23-11 (586-280)
A large vole-like rodent, similar in size to a small house cat, dark brownish in color with a long, naked, laterally compressed tail. Silvery gray below. Semi-aquatic and always seen near water. Common in suitable habitats throughout the Northwest except in southwestern British Columbia.

Muskrat trails in aquatic vegetation (Pend Oreille Co., Washington; E.J.L.)

Muskrat, with its lodge and feeding station

OLD WORLD RATS
AND MICE

The Old World rats and mice, as exemplified primarily by the Brown, or Norway, Rat and the House Mouse, occupy a unique position in the mammal fauna of the Pacific Northwest. First, they are exotics, introduced into the region by man. Second, they are literally commensals with man, practically eating at his table, as the word is defined, not by invitation, certainly, but intruding themselves nevertheless. These are the scavengers *par excellence* among our rodents, living mostly off of the leavings of human culture. Unattractive in appearance, furtive and nocturnal in habit, and a decided nuisance sanitation-wise, these animals are a curse to civilization and have been universally condemned and persecuted.

In certain places, as the grain fields of the Palouse country in eastern Washington, House Mice live in the open to a marked degree, often competing with the Montane Meadow Mouse and Common Deer Mouse for being the most abundant mouse species in such habitats. They are not found in forested or brushy places, as a rule, and probably their occurrence in the above-mentioned wheat fields depends on the abundance of scattered grain and relative proximity to farmsteads and settlements. If a house or building is not mouse-proof, it will have infestations of House Mice. When they are few in number, traps are effective in their control, as is the commercial poison "De-Con". The proper handling of wastes is very important. There is no reason why these animals should be present in a home or building if the above two remedies are utilized, that is, prevention of entry and prevention of food with a liberal sprinkling of traps and poison.

As a rule, the native rats and mice in the Northwest are of little trouble, as they mostly prefer to live under wild conditions. In forest homes, however, the Deer Mouse will come inside, but again, prevention of entry and traps will solve the problem. A more severe nuisance, however, is the pack rat in wilderness cabins, due to its greater propensity for damage and greater difficulty in trapping, especially if the animal has escaped from traps and become "trap-wise".

Mostly, we look upon wild mammals as interesting features of the natural scene or as sources of food. As the human population thickens up, however, these animals will come into increasingly close competition with man and the effects of environmental alteration on their welfare poses a series of value judgements that may not always be easy to make. In short, can we all live together? Fifty or seventy-five years ago, this was not a pressing problem in the Pacific Northwest. Anyone who is at all environmentally concerned at present recognizes that wild and domestic "togetherness" is becoming an increasing problem. The only solution is for the citizenry to become aware of the presence, distribution, habits, and values of the native mammals and to bear these items in mind when decisions regarding man-made changes in the natural scene are contemplated.

NORTHWEST SPECIES

ROOF RAT; BLACK RAT *Rattus rattus* 15 3/5 - 8 2/3 (390-216)
A large rat-like rodent, brownish or blackish in color, with a long nearly naked tail. Similar to the more common Brown Rat, but possesses a tail longer than the head and body. May occur in brownish, blackish, or white-bellied phases. Marshes, swamps, brush, and human habitations in the lowlands of western Washington and southwestern British Columbia.

BROWN RAT; NORWAY RAT *Rattus norvegicus* 14 3/4 - 7 1/2 (400-190)
A large, brownish, rat-like rodent with a long nearly-naked tail. Dirty white below. Primarily associated with the activities and habitats of man, but occasionally found in lowland marshes and along streams, throughout much of the Northwest.

HOUSE MOUSE *Mus musculus* 6 1/4 - 3 1/4 (160-82)
A small brownish-tan mouse, usually found in houses and buildings. Tail is long and naked, with characteristic ring-like scales. Lives in commensal relationship with man, but also occurs in feral condition in grain fields and occasionally along lowland streams and ponds. Throughout the Northwest, except the mountainous areas.

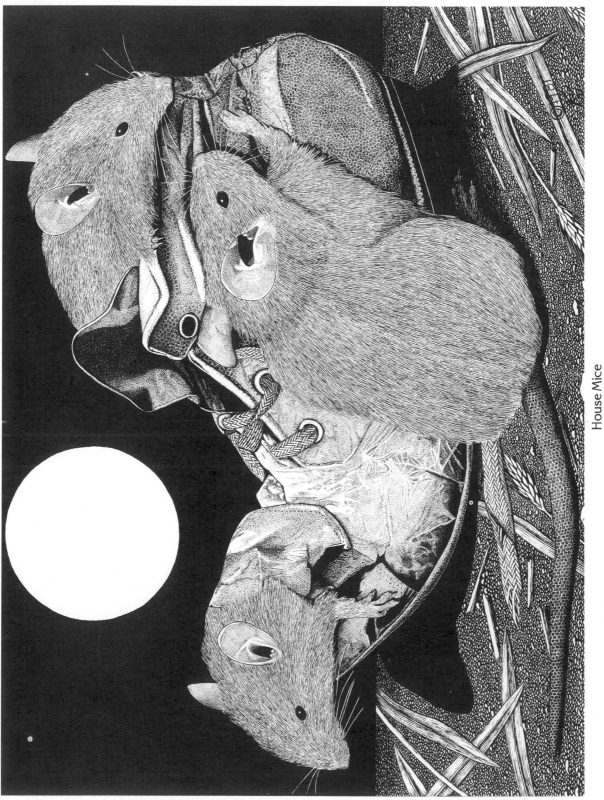

House Mice

JUMPING MICE

The jumping mice are small-bodied, long-tailed rodents with dusky orange backs and sides and whitish under parts. Locomotion is by a series of kangaroo-like leaps which carry them rapidly through or over the dense grass and herbage of their favorite habitats. They are commonly called "kangaroo mice", but mammalogists prefer to restrict that name to members of the genus *Microdipodops* of the Great Basin desert region. The family *Dipodidae,* to which our jumping mice belong, is a Holarctic one which includes the birch mice of northern and eastern Europe. The Pacific Northwest possesses three species of jumping mice, the Pacific Jumping Mouse (Cascades and western slope region), the Western Jumping Mouse (Rockies and interior) and the Meadow Jumping Mouse (northern and central British Columbia)....

Primarily nocturnal, these animals feed on in-sects, seeds, and berries and hibernate during the colder months of the year. In late summer, as any collector knows, jumping mice become very fat in preparation for their winter fasting. A thick layer of greasy fat forms beneath the skin and somewhat infiltrates the skin itself, making these mice difficult to prepare as specimens, as too much force in pulling the hide from the body will cause it to break. The proper procedure is not to remove all of the fat masses from the inside of the skin that will not come off easily, but to stuff the specimen, even though it is greasy, and allow it to dry and become stiff in the usual manner. Then, in a method recommended by the late Dr. George Hudson of Washington State University, immerse the dried specimen in two consecutive baths of white gasoline for 24 hours each, dry it out in plenty of sawdust, and blow the sawdust out of the fur with an air jet. This technique not only

Streamside habitat of the Jumping Mouse, Bog Lemming, and Heather Mouse (Priest Lake Country, northern Idaho; E.J.L.)

Pacific Jumping Mouse

removes the fat and grease but cleans the fur and kills any insect eggs that may be in it, and the air blowing fluffs up the cleaned fur nicely. In fact, all specimens should be so processed before they are incorporated into one's mammal collection. So much for our taxidermy lesson for today!

Shallow burrows or crannies under rocks or logs are used during the summer with deeper nests for hibernation. In reproduction, gestation is about 18 days with some five or six young born in the litter, and often two litters per summer season.

Larrison: MAMMALS OF THE NORTHWEST

NORTHWEST SPECIES

MEADOW JUMPING MOUSE *Zapus hudsonicus* 8 1/4 - 5 15/16 (215-127)
This species occurs in central and northern British Columbia, excluding the southwest coastal region and the southeastern corner of the province. Smaller size and range are distinctive. The head and body length of this species is usually less than 85 mm, while the same measurement in *Z.*

princeps is usually more than 85 mm. The latter species had a more montane distribution, as well.

WESTERN JUMPING MOUSE *Zapus princeps* 9 - 5 1/8 (230-130)
This species occurs throughout British Columbia, excepting the extreme southwest and northeast corners; in the northeast, extreme east, and southeast parts of Washington; in eastern and southcentral Oregon; and in all of Idaho.

PACIFIC JUMPING MOUSE *Zapus trinotatus* 9 2/5 - 5 2/5 (235-135)
The three Northwest jumping mice are very difficult to identify and separate from each other. They are best distinguished by technical cranial characters. Those persons using this book will find it easiest to name these three mice by considering their geographic ranges, as apparently there is little overlapping in distributional patterns (except in central and northern British Columbia). This particular species occurs in southwestern British Columbia, western Washington, and western Oregon, including the Olympic and Cascade Mountains and the Coast Range of western Oregon.

Porcupine

PORCUPINES

Porcupines are slow, rather stupid, timid animals, depending mainly on their spiny armor for protection, but always eager to get under cover or up a tree, or into a cave or cleft in the rocks for additional safety. Their only method of defense is to present the back with erect spines to the enemy and to strike upward and sideways with the powerful spiny tail, but in most cases this is ample defense. The quills are not thrown, as is commonly believed, but may be driven deep into an enemy by a blow of the tail, and if only lightly imbedded will work their way by means of their barbed points in through skin and flesh.

These animals are slow but industrious travelers, often leaving their lines of oval tracks in dusty trails for miles in a single night, wandering at random over deserts or open valley country, finding an abundance of plant food wherever they are, and taking advantage of any available cover for places to sleep during the day.

They have squeaky querulous voices, with many modifications to express anger, fear, or pain, and softer little squeals and grunts for friend-

Albino Porcupine (8 miles east of Kendrick, Idaho; J.R.C.)

ly feelings or entreaty. A treetop song has been reported in the mating season, but this needs further study. Generally, however, they are silent and by many are supposed to be voiceless.

They are excellent climbers and spend much of their time among the branches of large trees, where they are comparatively safe and where much of their winter food is obtained.

They do not hibernate even in the coldest winter weather and the deeper the snow the more easily available becomes their food of twigs and bark....

They are entirely vegetarian, and eat a wide range of plants. In summer most of their food is of low vegetation, clover, lupines, geranium, *Polygonum,* aster, parsnip, grass, many marsh plants, and a great variety of upland plants; also leaves and tips of numerous shrubs and small bushes, berries, fruits, and occasionally garden vegetables. They are very fond of apples and sweetpotatoes. In autumn and winter their food is largely twigs and bark of bushes and trees, and where the snow is deep almost entirely of tree bark, mostly lodgepole, yellow, sugar, limber, and whitebark pine, some Douglas spruce, apple, cherry, bullberry, and mountain-mahogany. The outer rough bark is scraped off and thrown down

A yellow-haired porcupine in the Juniper Forest of Eastern Washington (E.J.L.)

and only the green inner bark and cambium layer next to the wood are eaten. Their stomachs are very large and great quantities of coarse food are required to fill them. In 14 stomachs examined by Gabrielson the contents weighed from 1 to 3 pounds. In summer, their pellets are small and black, somewhat like those of sheep, but in winter they have large, oval, brown sawdust pellets, like those of the moose, only smaller, usually about an inch long.

Bailey: MAMMALS AND LIFE ZONES OF OREGON

NORTHWEST SPECIES

PORCUPINE *Erethizon dorsatum* 30 1/2 - 8 3/4 (775-220) The Porcupine is a large blackish or yellowish rodent covered with long hairs interspersed with short sharp spines (quills). The body is stocky and the animal's movements are slow and deliberate. Mostly occurs in forested and wooded areas, though occasionally found in open sagebrush and taiga forest and even tundra. Throughout the Northwest, excepting Vancouver Island and the Queen Charlottes.

Lowland truck gardens near water, a favorite habitat of the Nutria (King Co., Washington; E.J.L.)

NUTRIAS

The coypu (nutria) is a large octodont rodent about the size of a beaver and characterized by a round, almost-naked, rat-like tail, webbed hind feet, reddish-brown fur, and orange yellow incisors protruding through the furred lips. A most unusual character is the position of the mammae, which are on the back instead of the abdomen. It prefers a semi-aquatic habitat, occupying an ecological niche somewhat similar to the place taken by the muskrat in North America. The coypu has an extensive natural range, occurring in southeastern South America in coastal areas and in the larger rivers from about 15° south latitude in southern Brazil, Paraguay, and Bolivia to the Pacific coast of Tierra del Fuego (Osgood)....

Throughout much of their natural range in South America, the coypus prefer a semi-aquatic existence in swamps and marshes in and along rivers and lakes. However, in southern Chile and Tierra del Fuego, they are found mainly in the channels and bays separating the various islands off the coast. Here, according to Walter Eyerdam (in letter), "their habitat seems to be mostly in the estuaries of glacial fed streams and colonies of nutrias are often seen at certain times swimming amongst the floating ice blocks in the vicinity of glaciers." Apparently the coypu is equally at home in salt and fresh water.

The coastal region of Washington and Oregon with its many protected bays, tidal lagoons, and salt marshes and adjacent freshwater habitats furnishes a general ecological picture closely similar to that found in the more southern parts of the coypu's range on the coast of Chile. The southeastern coast of Alaska also provides ideal conditions for it.

In its South American home, the coypu feeds largely on the foliage and roots of aquatic plants and the vegetation on nearby banks. Mollusks and other shellfish living along the seashore are also eaten....

Esthetically, the coypu may represent an interesting addition to our wildlife, its large size and exotic appearance being very striking. Its nocturnal habits, however, prevent its being any more than casually seen — a fact attested by the Sammamish River colony [in Washington] being considered to be "beaver" by the local residents.

The coypu would have little value as a game and food animal in this country (future events may warrant a reexamination of this statement, however), though it is used as such by the natives in South America.

It is the habit of the coypu in South America to burrow extensively in banks along water in search of roots and nesting sites. It is conceivable that this activity could be potentially very injurious to banks and earthen constructions along waterways if the animals become very numerous in Washington and Oregon. In this connection, Wire writes that "...we do not consider them a valuable fur animal as they do considerable damage by boring at dikes and levees, doing more harm even than muskrats or beaver....We do not feel that they are desirable animals to have in this state [Oregon] and would be glad to get rid of them". The coypu may also represent an important predator on agricultural activities near its aquatic haunts. This would hold true especially in the Puget Sound area where practically all of the truck gardens supplying the large cities are located in river valleys where habitats favorable for coypus are plentiful.

Larrison: Article in THE MURRELET

NORTHWEST SPECIES

NUTRIA; COYPU *Myocastor coypus* 34 1/3 - 11 4/5 (857-295)

This species is a large beaver-sized rodent, with reddish-brown fur, webbed hind feet, and a round naked tail. Prefers semi-aquatic habitats as provided by swamps, marshes, and stream and lake margins. All individuals found in the Northwest are escapees or descendants of escapees from fur farms. Occurs mostly in western Washington and Oregon and extreme southwestern mainland of British Columbia with scattered populations elsewhere.

Coypus

DOGS

Besides these sounds [wolf howls] as a means of intercommunication, Wolves use the example, already set forth, and scents.

The scent method of communicating ideas I made the subject of an article in *Forest & Stream,* Jan. 23, 1897 (pp. 64-65). I reproduce the substance of it here.

SMELL-POWER. It is well known that not only each species of animal, but that each individual has its own peculiar smell, conclusive evidence of which is found in the fact that a good Dog has no difficulty in following his master through a crowd, or keeping to the track of the animal he is hunting, though it be crossed by the tracks of many others.

It is further known that, even though it always retains its individuality, this personal odour varies with the condition of the animal. Thus a Horse smells strong after exercise; Canada grouse and Snowshoe Hares smell of spruce or cedar when they feed on these; a Mink smells different when angry; Dogs in ill-health become malodorous; Deer in rut become offensively strong-smelling; a female animal in rut is recognized afar by the scent.

ODOUR-GLANDS. In many species ad-ditional effect is given to the body-scent by the development of special glands which secrete a strong odour. These glands are usually situated in a part which is habitually brought in contact with the ground or the vegetation. Thus, in a Musk-deer they are on the side of the belly; in the Peccary, on the back; in our common Deer, on the tarsus, between the toes, and in the lachrymal fossa. In some animals, however, the contact with the ground is secured in a different way. The glands are situated within the anal and preputial orifices, so that the natural excretions *in transitu* bear with them the taint which reveals so much to the next passer-by of the same species.

How much of these informational odours is supplied by the protometra, is not yet known. The protometra or protometric gland is, according to Chaveau, a small pouch present in all domestic animals, and sometimes double, which secretes a fluid that is thrown into the urethra through a very small orifice near the *Verumontanum.*

George Fleming, the English editor, adds to this that the gland is not a gland in the ordinary

"Killer", Jim Christensen's pet Coyote (Kendrick, Idaho; J.R.C.)

Red Fox (northern British Columbia; E.J.L.)

Coyotes: a mother and pups in serenade

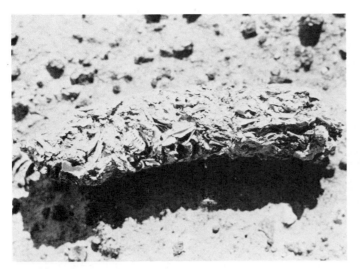

Bone-filled Coyote scat (Hanford Atomic Reservation, Washington; J.R.C.)

sense of the term, but is certainly the rudiment of the duct that develops into the uterus of the female. It is also called the *prostatic utricle* or *sinus pocularis.*

WOLF WIRELESS. In order that the second animal may find the depot of intelligence quickly, it is necessary that his discovery of the place be not left to chance; and, incredible as it may seem at first sight, there is abundant proof that the whole of a region inhabited by Wolves is laid out in signal stations or intelligence depots. Usually there is one at each mile or less, varying much with the nature of the ground. The marks of these depots, or odour-posts, are various; a stone, a tree, a bush, a Buffalo skull, a post, a mound, or any similar object serves, provided only that it is conspicuous on account of its colour or position; usually it is more or less isolated, or else prominent by being at the crossing of two trails.

Now, a man returning to town goes at once to his hotel or club, glances over the last three or four names on the register, adds his own, then makes a more thorough inspection. And the behavior of an animal arrived at an odour-post is precisely the same. It approaches, hastily sniffs the post, adds its own odour, then makes a more thorough investigation. The attention that Dogs pay to lamp-posts in town is precisely the same habit, a trifle overdeveloped through idleness, etc., but it will serve to illustrate. I have many times seen a Dog approach the post, sniff, then growl,

register, growl again, and, with bristling mane and glowing eyes, scratch fiercely with his hind-feet, and walk off very stiffly, glancing back from time to time.

Again, it is common to see a Dog, after the preliminaries, become keenly interested, trot about the vicinity, and come back again and again to make his own record more evident. At other times one sees the animal, suddenly aroused by the news, take up a recent trail or fly to the next signal post, and so continue in pursuit of whatever it was that was sensed.

REGISTERING. Wolves do precisely the same, but I believe they carry it to a higher pitch, and there can be no doubt that a newly arrived Wolf is quickly aware of the visit that has recently been paid to the signal post — by a personal friend or foe, by a female in search of a mate, a young or old, sick or well, hungry, hunted, or gorged beast. From the trail he learns further the direction whence it came and whither it went. Thus the main items of news essential to his life are obtained by the system of signal posts.

Every man who has hunted or trapped Wolves knows how soon they divine a new campaign against them. The word is passed around (on the odour-posts partly), and the Wolves move to a less troubled neighborhood, showing a wonderfully effective system of communication among these freebooters.

Seton: LIVES OF GAME ANIMALS

Gray Fox (J.W.T.)

105

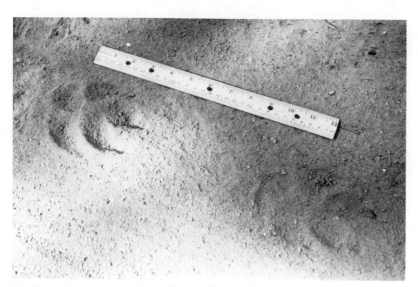

Wolf tracks in road dust (Pend Oreille Co., Washington; E.J.L.)

Bloody trails at a Wolf kill of a White-tailed Deer near Larrison's cabin in Pend Oreille Co., Washington (E.J.L.)

Wolf photographed at Northwest Trek (J.R.C.)

White-tailed Deer killed by Coyote pack (Pend Oreille Co., Washington; E.J.L.)

NORTHWEST SPECIES

COYOTE *Canis latrans* 51 · 13 3/4 (1,300-350)
A slender, medium-sized, wild dog, grayish brown with reddish on the legs, feet, and ears. Bushy tail and large pointed ears. Tail carried down when animal is running. Occurs throughout the Northwest (except coastal British Columbia and Vancouver and Queen Charlotte Islands) in a variety of desert, semi-forested, forested, agricultural, and urban areas.

GRAY WOLF *Canis lupus* 59 · 15 (1,500-400)
A very large grayish or blackish wild dog with heavy muzzle, long legs, and bushy tail. Lighter on sides and muzzle. The largest of the wild dogs and usually larger than most domestic breeds. Appears "long legged". Scattered to rare in forests and mountainous areas south of the Canadian border. More numerous north of that line.

RED FOX *Vulpes vulpes* 39-16 (1,000-400)
A slender, small- to medium-sized dog usually reddish in color with white belly and black feet and a conspicuous bushy tail. Some individuals are black with white frosting over the back, solid black (but with white tip on tail), or yellowish red with crossed dusky patches along the back and over the shoulders. In forested and semi-forested areas of much of the Northwest, except the rainforests and desert regions.

KIT FOX *Vulpes velox* 28 1/2 · 15 1/4 (725-250)
Small buffy-colored fox with white under parts and black tip to tail. Pelage is soft and silky. Open desert areas in southeastern Oregon and southern Idaho. Sparse to rare in occurrence.

GRAY FOX *Urocyon cinereoargenteus* 40 2/5 · 15 1/4 (1,030-390)
Same size or smaller than the Red Fox, but with dark gray upper parts (dark midline), reddish brown under parts (white throat and belly). Legs are shorter and claws more strongly curved than in the Red Fox. Open woods and brushy or rocky places in western Oregon.

Two color phases of the Red Fox

Kit Fox

109

Gray Fox and Spotted Skunk

BEARS

First the brown, white, or grisly (grizzly) bear which seems to be of the same family (the same species, *Ursus horribilis*), with an accidental variation of color only, inhabits the timbered parts of the Rocky Mountains. These are rarely found on the westerly side, and are more common below the Rocky Mountains, on the plains or on their borders, amidst copses of brush and underwood, and near the water-courses. We are unable to learn that they inhabit at all the woody country bordering on the coast as far in the interior as the (Cascade) range of mountains which passes the Columbia between the Great Falls and rapids (Cascades) of that river.

Lewis and Clark: COUES' EDITION OF THE JOURNALS

The grizzly bear is the most notable discovery made in zoology by Lewis and Clark. Their accounts are very full, as we have already seen, and shall see again in several places. This bear was found to be so numerous and so fierce, especially in the Upper Missouri region, as to more than once endanger the lives of the party, and form an impediment to the progress of the Expedition. Our authors carefully distinguish the grizzly, in all its color-variations, from the black bear (*Ursus americanus*); they are at pains to describe it minutely and repeatedly, laying special stress, for specific characters, upon its great size in all its

dimensions, its general build and the form of the feet and claws, the peculiarity of the scrotum, together with the inability of this species to climb trees, its great ferocity, and its remarkable tenacity of life. Their records are for the most part judicious and pertinent, establishing the species as distinct from the black bear; and have been confirmed by subsequent investigators. The differences had long been known to the Indians....the fact that the grizzly in all its variety of color is different from the black bear, some color varieties of which latter are nevertheless like some of those of the grizzly.... The adjectives "grisly" and "grizzly" are used indiscriminately by our authors; but it may be observed that *grisly* means horrible, terrible, fearful, and the like, while *grizzly* means of a grizzled

Grizzly Bear (Olympic Game Farm; J.R.C.)

111

Grizzly Bear

gray color. Both designations are pertinent; the former is rendered by the Latin word *horribilis*, and is preferable, because it applies to all the color-variations of the animal; but "grizzly" is the adjective most in use....

The black bear, like the grizzly, runs into color-variation, the best marked of which is a light reddish-brown; which variety is known as the "cinnamon" bear (*Ursus cinnamomus*). A bear of this kind closely resembles, as far as color goes, some of the brownest varieties of the grizzly — a fact which has caused great though needless confusion. It is only necessary to remember that there are some "cinnamon" bears which are a variety of the species *Ursus americanus* and other "cinnamon" bears which are a variety of the species *Ursus horribilis*. The common black bear was known to science long before the grizzly was discovered.

> Coues' note in his edition of the
> Lewis and Clark Journals

...Captain Lewis, who was on shore with one hunter, met about eight o'clock two white [grizzly] bears of the strength and ferocity of this animal the Indians had given us dreadful accounts. They never attacked him but in parties of six or eight persons, and even then are often defeated with a loss of one or more of their party. Having no weapons but bows and arrows and the bad guns with which the traders supply them, they are obliged to approach very near to the bear; as no wound except through the head or heart is mortal, they frequently fall a sacrifice if they miss their aim....Such is the terror which he has inspired, that the Indians who go in quest of him paint themselves and perform all the superstitious rites customary when they make war on a neighboring nation. Hitherto these bears we had seen did not appear desirous of encountering us; but although to a skillful rifleman the danger is very much diminished, yet the white bear is still a terrible animal. On approaching these two, both Captain Lewis and the hunter fired, and each wounded a bear. One of them made his escape; the other turned upon Captain Lewis and pursued him 70 to 80 yards, but being badly wounded the bear could not run so fast as to prevent him from reloading his piece, which he again aimed at him, and a third shot from the hunter brought him to

Sleeping Big Brown Bear (southern Alaska; E.J.L.)

Mother Grizzly Bear and cubs (J.W.T.)

Black Bear begging in Yellowstone National Park (E.J.L.)

Black Bear Cubs

the ground. He was a male, not quite full grown, and weighed about 300 pounds. The legs were somewhat longer than those of the black bear, and the talons and tushes much larger and longer....Its color is a yellow-brown; the eyes are small, black, and piercing; the front of the fore legs near the feet is usually black, and the fur is finer, thicker, and deeper than that of the black bear. Add to which, it is a more ferocious animal, and very remarkable for the wounds which it will bear without dying....

Captain Clark and one of the hunters [Drewyer] met this evening the largest brown bear [grizzly bear, *Ursus horribilis*] we have seen. As they fired he did not attempt to attack, but fled with a most tremendous roar; and such was his extraordinary tenacity of life that, although five balls passed through his lungs and he had five other wounds, he swam more than half across the river to a sand-bar, and survived 20 minutes. He weighed between 500 and 600 pounds at least, and measured 8 feet 7 1/2 inches from the nose to the extremity of the hind feet, 5 feet 10 1/2 inches round the breast, 3 feet 11 inches round the neck, 1 foot 11 inches round the middle of the foreleg, and his talons, five on each foot, were 4 3/8 inches in length....

Captain Lewis, who had forgotten to reload his rifle, was intently watching him [a buffalo which Lewis had just shot] fall, when he behold a large brown bear which was stealing on him unperceived, and was already within 20 steps. In the first moment of surprise, he lifted his rifle, but remembering instantly that it was not charged, and that he had no time to reload, he felt that there was no safety but in flight. It was in the open level plain — not a bush or tree within 300 yards,

the bank of the river sloping and not more than three feet high, so that there was no possible mode of concealment. Captain Lewis therefore thought of retreating in a quick walk, as fast as the bear advanced toward the nearest tree; but as soon as he turned, the bear ran open-mouthed and at full speed. Captain Lewis ran about 80 yards, but in finding that the animal gained on him fast, it flashed on his mind that, by getting into the water to such a depth that the bear would be obliged to attack him swimming, there was still some chance of his life; he therefore turned short, plunged into the river about waist-deep, and facing about presented the point of his espontoon....

Lewis and Clark: COUES' EDITION OF THE JOURNALS

NORTHWEST SPECIES

BLACK BEAR *Ursus americanus* 69 · 5 (1,750-128)
The common bear of the Pacific Northwest. Usually blackish in most regions, but more commonly brownish in the interior. Other color phases are cinnamon, blond, blue-gray, and white. The toe nails are short and black and there is no shoulder hump in this species. Forested, wooded, or swampy habitats throughout much of the Northwest. To be commonly found in burns and subalpine areas during the "huckleberry season".

GRIZZLY BEAR *Ursus arctos* 75 · 6 3/4 (1,912-172)
Much larger than the Black Bear, with a grizzled brownish pelage, long yellow or brown claws, and a conspicuous hump on the shoulders. Some bears of the extreme northwest coast of British Columbia are much larger than the ordinary Grizzly and are called "big brown bears", possibly representing a separate species. The Grizzly occurs scatteringly to rarely in open places in the Cascades, Okanogan Highlands of Washington, and Bitterroots of Idaho. Somewhat more numerous in British Columbia. Prefers subalpine and open grass areas. A most dangerous mammal and not to be approached.

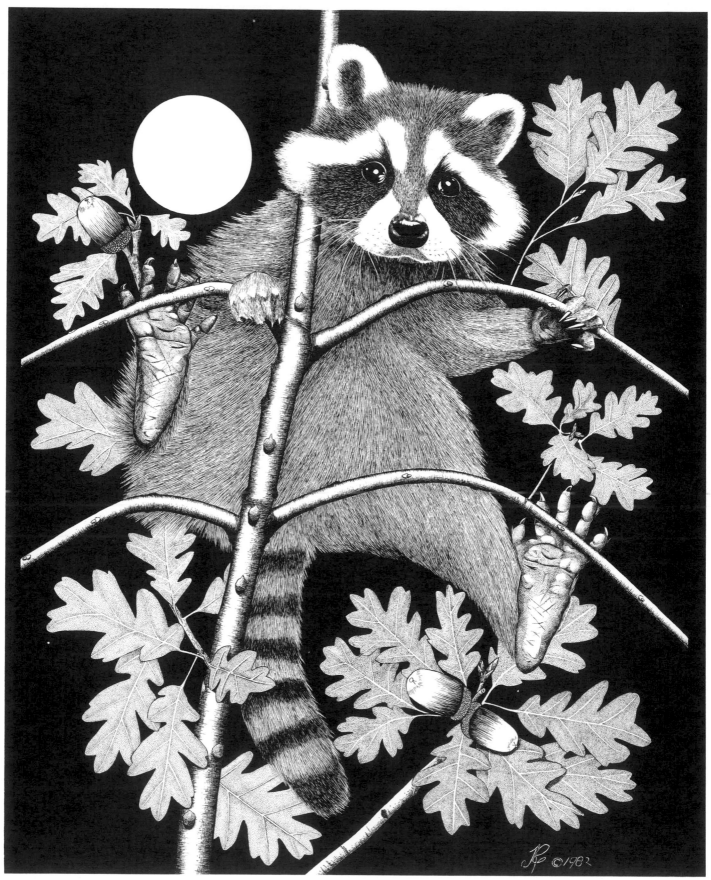

Raccoon

PROCYONIDS

The Raccoon is a creature of woodland edges, preferably hardwood. Dense coniferous forests do not please it; one reason being that hollow trees are essential to its well-being. It does occasionally lodge in rocky crannies, even in bank burrows, but this is exceptional, and imposed by the absence of more congenial quarters. No matter what its daytime residence is, its nightly prowling is always close to the water. So that we look for it with certainty in all temperate parts of America, where big timber and water abound; and we are perfectly safe in omitting from the map an arid region where timber is scarce, and running water unknown....

The Raccoon is quite omnivorous. Frogs, fish, flesh, fowl, eggs, reptiles, insects, shell-fish, fruit, nuts, grain, vegetables, and sweets are acceptable fare with him; not equally so, but all welcome at all times.

It may occasionally rob the nest of woodpecker, squirrel, or other tree-dweller, but such must not be considered its normal habit of life. By far the greatest bulk of its food is taken on or near the ground.

In a wild state, the summer-long main support of the Coon is frogs. In catching them by night, it is singularly expert, and when the frog takes refuge in the muddy bottom, the Coon, with wonderfully dexterous, tactile fingers, gropes after it. Of course, it cannot smell them under water, or see them in the mud. Leaving the enterprise entirely to its paws, its eyes may scan the woods and shores in a vacant way, but its mind is in touch with its finger-tips, and the frog that escapes them must indeed be worthy to live, and father a superior race....

As Merriam says: "They overturn stones, and catch the crayfish that lurk beneath, and also gather the fresh-water mussels (*Unio* and *Anodon*) that live on sandy and muddy bottoms. They also catch and devour the hapless fish that chance to get detained in any of the little pools along-shore, but are unable to dive and pursue their prey under water, like the Otter and Mink".

In parts of the South where crayfish live in the levees and embankments, the Raccoon does good service in destroying these troublesome crustaceans.

Pennant describes this animal as particularly fond of oysters, and says it "will watch the opening of the shell, dexterously put in its paw, and tear out the contents; sometimes the oyster suddenly closes, catches the thief and detains it till drowned by the return of the tide."

H.B. Warren, in his "Enemies of Poultry", assembles many testimonies of farmers, to show that the Raccoon not only kills poultry at times, but is a persistent fisherman, and very successful where shallow water leaves trout, etc., more or less at his mercy, in pools that represent the low tide of streams.

In the Southern States, its coat may change to a less substantial style, but its appetite for all nutritious dainties is the same. Bachman details its watching of "the soft-shelled turtle, when she is about to deposit her eggs, for which purpose she leaves the water and, crawling on to the white sand-bar, digs a hole and places them underneath the heated surface. Quickly does the rogue dig up the elastic ova, although ever so carefully covered, and appropriate them to his own use, notwithstanding the efforts of the luckless turtle to conceal them."

"Sometimes by the margin of a pond, shrouded, or crouching among tall weeds and grasses, Grimalkin-like, the Raccoon lies still as death, waiting with patience for some ill-fated duck that may come within his reach. No Negro on a plantation knows with more accuracy when the corn (maize) is juicy and ready for the connoisseur in roasting ears, and he does not require the aid of fire to improve its flavour, but attacks it more voraciously than the Squirrel or the blackbird, and is the last to quit the cornfield...and although it generally visits the cornfields at night sometimes feeds on the green corn during the day; we have seen it thus employed during the heat of summer."

117

Ringtail

Although the frog-pond and the corn-patch supply its choicest foods, the Coon is not averse to a fat fowl. Some individuals, indeed, seem to give way to the chicken habit, and riot to the henhouse night after night, killing first one fowl and then a dozen at a time, until they fall into the power of the barn-fowl's proper guardian....

These, however, are abnormal individuals and are not to be considered representative of the race. It is possible that, like most Lords of the Forest, its principal revenue is derived from Mice, which are available when frogs and fruit are not.

Summing up its dietary, there is nothing in it, except occasional thefts of corn and fowl, to blacklist this creature on the farm book; and these little sins are so completely offset by its usefulness as a fur-bearer and beast of the chase, that most persons are glad to hear that the Coon is spreading, if not actually increasing, in America.

Seton: LIVES OF GAME ANIMALS

Raccoon photographed at Northwest Trek (J.R.C.)

NORTHWEST SPECIES

RINGTAIL *Bassariscus astutus* 28 · 14 3/4 (700-370)
A small, slender, cat-like animal, buffy in color, and with a long ringed tail (black and white rings). The ears are large and erect. Strongly nocturnal. Occurs in rocky and brushy desert habitats in southwestern Oregon with one record in extreme eastern Idaho near the Wyoming border.

RACCOON *Procyon lotor* 35 1/2 · 11 (905-280)
A stocky medium-sized carnivore with grizzled blackish-gray upper parts, black mask over the eyes and cheeks, and conspicuously ringed bushy tail. The toes are long and finger-like. The animal usually has a conspicuous hump in the back. Prefers woods and brushy areas near fresh or salt water throughout the Pacific Northwest, excepting all of British Columbia but the southernmost part.

Raccoon tracks (E.J.L.)

119

Mink

MUSTELIDS

The Wolverine, Carcajou, or — as the Indians of Washington call it — the Mountain Devil, is quite at home in the Elk River mountains [of British Columbia], but his shrewdness is so great that he is seldom seen outside a trap. Unquestionably, this is the most interesting small mammal of the northwest. In some places it is called the Skunk-"Bear."

If you meet a strange trapper and desire to take a measure of his moral leanings, ask his opinion of the moral character and mental capacity of the Wolverine. I have heard trappers solemnly declare that no matter how much any one may malign this particular devil, its character always is much blacker than it can be painted.

The Wolverine is the largest, the strongest, most vicious and most cunning member of the Marten Family. In comparison with the size of its body, its teeth are of enormous size and power. It is about as large as a fox terrier, and ten times as savage as a bull-dog. It is built on the plan and specifications of a Malay sun-bear, and has the same evil eye, wedge-shaped head, splay feet and truculent manner. It has long hair, ivory-white claws, and a mean-looking tail that looks as if it had been cut off half way, and healed up with a

River Otters (mill pond at Kendrick, Idaho; J.R.C.)

wisp end. The animal runs with its tail down, but when it stops to look back, up goes the tail, skunk-like. In spying out the land, a Wolverine often rises high on its hind legs....

The Wolverine is a fairly good climber, and game hung in a tree is not safe from its destructive jaws. Mr. J.W. Tyrrell once outwitted the wolverines of the Barren Grounds by erecting a cache on four very high posts, then trimming the posts and peeling off all the bark, after which he nailed six cod-hooks to each post. The Wolverines tried very hard to climb up to that cache, but failed....

A Wolverine will follow the trail of a trapper, visit every one of his marten traps (or any others, for that matter), spring every trap, steal every bait, and take out every marten that has been caught. If the marten is not dead, it is killed and torn out of the trap; and if dead and frozen, it is seized by the body and violently jerked until the trapped leg is torn off the body, and the skin spoiled. The dead body will then be carried some distance, a neat hole will be dug straight down into the snow for perhaps two feet, and the dead marten is cached at the bottom. Then the snow is replaced in the hole, tamped down and neatly smoothed over on

Fisher, photographed at Northwest Trek (J.R.C.)

121

Marten

the surface, after which the Wolverine defiles the snow over the grave, and goes his wicked way.

By these signs, the trapper knows where to dig for his stolen marten. J.R. Norboe once recovered four martens out of six that had been stolen by a Wolverine on one line of traps.

In the Elk River Valley, C.L. Smith once had about seventy miles of traps, and every mile of his lines was gone over by Wolverines. He said, "They caused me a great deal of loss, and at last they nearly drove me crazy." He once set a trap for a Wolverine, and put behind it a moose skull bearing some flesh. The Wolverine came in the night, started in at a point well away from the trap, dug a tunnel through six feet of snow, fetched up at the head, — well behind the trap, — and dragged it in triumph through his tunnel and away.

The female Wolverine has four young at a birth, and they are born in December. The mothers are more fierce and troublesome in February and March than either earlier or later, for it is during these months that they are required to work hardest in feeding their young.

Contrary to the statements of the earlier writings upon the Wolverine, the three trappers in our party united in expressing the opinion that this animal is not a gluttonous feeder, and that the amount of food it consumes is proportionately no greater than that of other members of the Marten Family, — marten, fisher, mink, otter, etc. The Edwards Brothers, animal showmen, have today a captive Wolverine which they have kept for twelve years, and its daily ration of meat is only half a pound.

To a trapper, the Wolverine's crowning injury and unpardonable insult is the invasion of his cabin, during his absence. Then it is, with the trapper far from home, and his all-too-scanty winter's store of flour, bacon, coffee, and sugar laid bare and at his mercy, that the eternal cussedness of *Gulo luscus* rises to the sublime. He rips open every sack and parcel, scatters flour, coffee, sugar and grease in one chaotic mass upon the cabin floor, and wallows in it, with ghoulish glee. He goes to the bunk, and with fiendish persistence tears the blankets to shreds. The stove is about the only thing in the cabin that goes unscathed. At the last, he defiles to the utmost every edible that he cannot carry away, and departs.

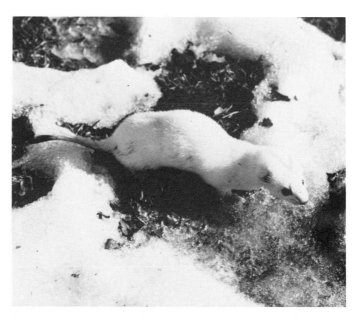

Short-tailed Weasel (Rimrock Reservoir, Yakima Co., Washington; J.R.C.)

Short-tailed Weasel tracks (Pend Oreille Co., Washington; E.J.L.)

123

Long-tailed Weasel in summer pelage

124

Subalpine habitat of the Marten (E.J.L.)

Wolverine tracks (Yellowstone National Park; E.J.L.)

Charlie Smith tells with much fervor how he got even with a Wolverine which made several unsuccessful attempts to raid his cabin. One morning before starting out on his trap-line, he buried a trap directly in front of his cabin door, and set the door slightly ajar. Just inside the door, he placed some meat. Then, on the roof-peak of his cabin, at one end of the structure he rigged a balanced pole, like a well-sweep, drew down the small end, and under it very carelessly hung a deer's head, in a small tree. Directly under the head he set a trap, and attached it to the end of the pole.

He figured out the mental process of the Wolverine in this wise: He will suspect the trap in front of the door, and avoid it. But he will discover the deer's head, and say, "Aha! This fellow has forgotten that I am about!" and straightway he will stand up on his hind legs and reach for the head, with his front feet against the tree.

The Wolverine came, and saw, and thought, and did precisely as the trapper had figured out that he would; and that night when Charlie came home, he found his cunning enemy hanging high in the air, "and dead as a wedge."

Hornaday: CAMP FIRES IN THE CANADIAN ROCKIES

Striped Skunk (Pend Oreille Co., Washington; E.J.L.)

Wolverine (photographed at Northwest Trek; J.R.C.)

NORTHWEST SPECIES

MARTEN *Martes americana* 24 - 6 3/4 (600-170)
Large brownish or reddish-yellow weasel-like animal. Pelage lighter below with a yellow or orange patch on the chin and a grayish head. Fur is soft and fluffy. Coniferous forests, mostly of the mountains. Moderately numerous, particularly in the lower alpine areas.

FISHER *Martes pennanti* 40-16 (1,000-400)
Similar to the Marten, but much larger and darker. Under parts, rump, legs, and tail are blackish. The tail is long and bushy. Dense coniferous forests of the Northwest, except on Vancouver Island. Uncommon to rare, except more numerous on the Olympic Peninsula.

SHORT-TAILED WEASEL; ERMINE *Mustela erminea* males: 8 5/8 - 2 3/10 (220-56); females: 7 7/8 - 2 (197-50)
Medium-sized weasel. In summer, brown above and pale yellowish white below; in winter, all white except for black tip on tail. Occurs in a variety of habitats throughout the Northwest. Common.

LEAST WEASEL *Mustela nivalis* males: 7 11/16 - 15/16 (196-34) females: 6 7/8 - 1 (176-25)
A very small weasel. In summer, brown above and white below. In winter, completely white, except for a few black hairs at the tip of the tail. Northeastern and central British Columbia in open to semi-open woods.

LONG-TAILED WEASEL *Mustela frenata* males: 16 1/2 - 6 1/8 (420-157); females: 12 7/8 - 5 1/2 (328-37)
A large weasel, similar in coloration to the Short-tailed Weasel, both in winter and summer. Lowland population west of the Cascades may not become completely white in winter. Northwest states and central and southern British Columbia (excepting Vancouver Island), in a variety of habitats.

MINK *Mustela vison* 21 1/2 - 6 7/8 (548-175)
A large weasel-like animal, rich brownish in color with white patches on the skin and throat. Tail only moderately bushy. Fairly common in habitats near water throughout most of the Pacific Northwest.

WOLVERINE *Gulo gulo* 40 - 8 1/4 (1,000-210)
The size of a small bear and somewhat bear-like in appearance. Dark brownish black above with two yellowish stripes along upper sides from shoulders to rump and tail. Under parts dark, marked with yellowish or white throat patches. Light markings on face. Feet are short and the weasel-like humping gait are distinctive. Scattered throughout the Northwest, except for the desert regions. Probably mostly to be seen in forested mountainous areas. More numerous in British Columbia.

BADGER *Taxidea taxus* 29 1/2 - 4 7/8 (780-125)
A flat, short-legged, heavy-bodied carnivore with a yellowish-gray body marked with black and white stripes on the head. Feet black. Occurs in open to semi-open country in the arid to semi-arid regions of the Northwest.

SPOTTED SKUNK *Spilogale putorius* 16 1/2 - 5 1/2 (450-140)
A small, black, plump carnivore with white spots on forehead and cheeks, white stripes on the sides and back, and a white tassle on the end of the tail. Occurs in brushy and rocky habitats and near farmsteads through much of the Northwest except northeastern Washington, northern Idaho, and eastern and central British Columbia.

STRIPED SKUNK *Mephitis mephitis* 28 - 11 3/4 (710-300)
A large skunk with shiny black fur, marked with a broad white stripe down each side of the back from the top of the head to the base of the tail. A narrow white stripe down the center of the head between the eyes. Occurs in a variety of habitats, mostly near water, throughout most of the Northwest excepting Vancouver Island and western British Columbia.

RIVER OTTER *Lutra canadensis* 45 1/3 - 18 1/8 (1,150-460)
A very large weasel-like mammal, brownish black above and somewhat lighter below (with a silky sheen). Legs and ears short with the feet webbed and the fur short and dense. The tail broadens into the lower back. Occurs near water (fresh or salt) throughout the Northwest. Seems to prefer to live along the larger rivers where trash fish are abundant.

SEA OTTER *Enhydra lutris* 60 - 12 2/5 (1,530-310)
A large light to dark brownish or even blackish mustelid frosted with whitish hairs. Head and neck are lighter — sometimes almost whitish. Ears very small, hind feet are webbed, and the tail is short and thick. Entirely marine. Uncommon to rare at several places along the ocean coast where it has been re-introduced after having been extirpated. Spends most of its time swimming and floating at the surface in the salt water.

Badger (near Pegosa Springs, Archuleta Co., Colorado; J.R.C.)

127

Spotted Skunk

Badger and Striped Skunk

129

Sea Otter on land (Woodland Park Zoo, Seattle, Washington; E.J.L.)

Sea Otter (Seattle Aquarium; J.R.C.)

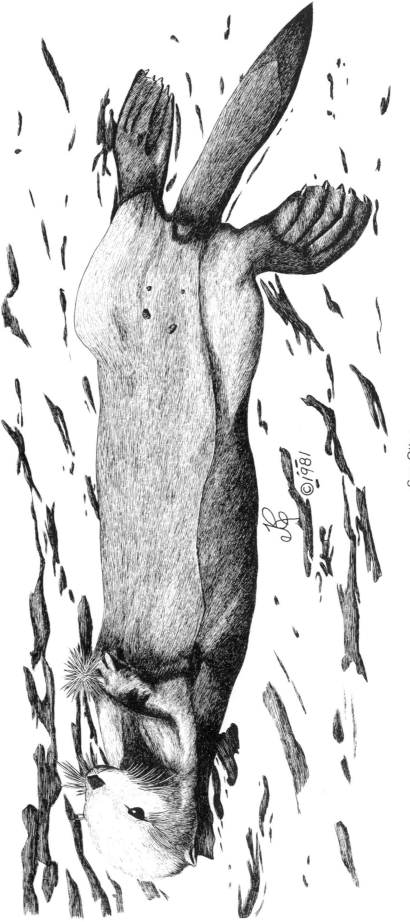

Sea Otter

131

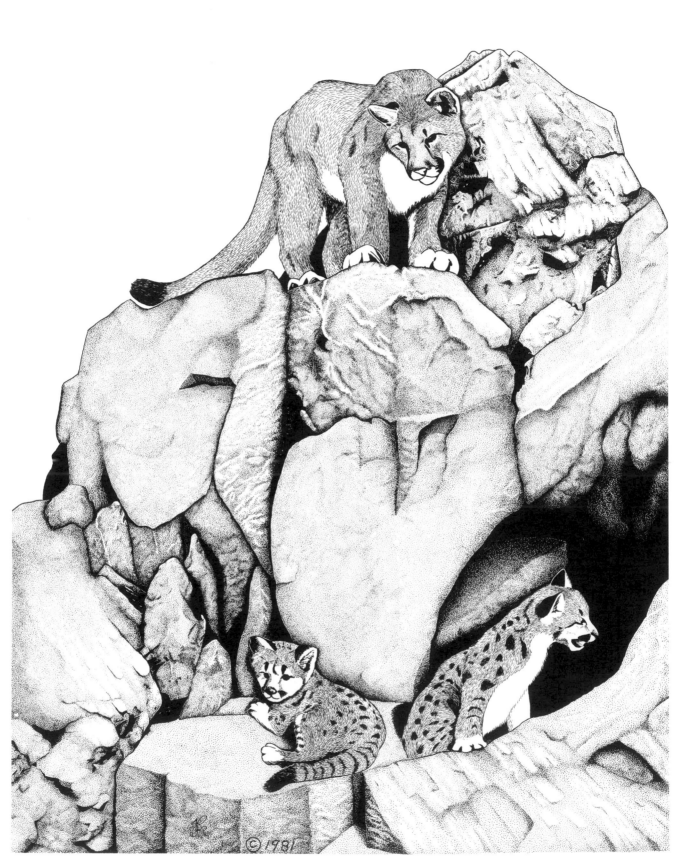

Cougar Mother and Kittens

CATS

...On looking through the glasses my surprise was great, for pressed into the snow was an apparently dead sheep [Dall's Sheep], its head covered with blood, and crouched beside it was a lynx, intently watching me. I pushed the kodak into its case and unslung the rifle, while the lynx ran a hundred feet up the creek and disappeared among the crags. Hurrying forward, I saw it climb among the rocks with easy agility and again disappear. Reaching a point opposite where it had last been seen I carefully scrutinized the crags and finally spied it standing on the edge of a cliff, looking down at me. Its color and markings caused it to blend almost completely with the rocks. It was at least a hundred and fifty yards above me, and in order to improve the chance of hitting it, I slowly moved back across the creek to a high sloping bank where, reclining against a snowdrift and with elbow on my knees, I could obtain a good rest for an aim. The lynx remained motionless, but at the shot dropped over the cliff, bounding and rolling until it fell over a small precipice into a gully, down which it slid swiftly to the creek bed. The bullet had struck it in the neck.

Picking up the lynx, I carried it over to the sheep, coiled it as nearly as possible in the posi-

Cougar (J.W.T.)

tion in which it had first been seen, and photographed it. On examining the sheep I was shocked to find the head completely covered with bloody foam, and warm blood still streaming from the eyes. It lay as though dead, the forelegs doubled under and the head pushed into the snow. Grasping a horn, I lifted the head, when to my horror the poor animal struggled up on its forefeet, tottered a moment, and sank to its knees. I quickly dispatched it. Both eyes had been completely gouged out, and surrounding them were deep gashes. The signs on the snow were unmistakable, revealing exactly what had happened only a few moments before I came to witness the end of this horrible tragedy. At great risk I scaled the rocks three hundred feet up to the point where the attack had been made.

The lynx had come down from above, its tracks showing that it had crept along, crossing ravines, crouching on a rock or in the snow, all the time watching the sheep. It finally lay in wait on a jutting ledge over a gully about six feet deep. The sheep — a young ram — fed along unconcious of the danger, and as it stepped into the gully just below the lynx, the lynx had leapt onto the centre of its back, fastening its teeth above and below the

Cougar tracks on a dusty road (Pend Oreille Co., Washington; E.J.L.)

133

Face of a Bobcat

Bobcat and Yellow-bellied Marmot

left eye, both rows sinking with a firm grip well into the bone. The ram had struggled down the gulch, endeavoring without success to throw off its enemy. The snow in the hollow was churned and bloody, and here and there on the rocks at the sides were patches of blood, where the ram had struck its head. Then, where it had slid and struggled downward for three hundred feet to the creek bed, the snow for a space twenty-five feet square was trampled and bloody. The ram had been thrown several times during the struggle and undoubtedly the lynx had kept chewing about its left eye. It was evident that the lynx at one time had lost its hold on the left eye and had then fastened its teeth about the right eye, which had been completely bitten out — though the gouged space about it was not so large as that about the left. The left ear was entirely torn off. Finally the ram, from shock, loss of blood, and exhaustion, had sunk down in the position where I found it, and where it would shortly have died.

A careful examination of the ram revealed that only claw punctures were on the skin. Of these, there were eleven a little below and behind the left ear, all close together; there were three just

below the right shoulder, four deep ones an inch to the right of the spine in the middle of the back, and three ten inches farther back, just to the left of the spine. The flesh under these punctures showed that the claws had been more or less buried in it. It was evident therefore that the lynx had landed on the back of the ram and buried its left fore claws in the neck below and behind the left ear, its right fore claws just below the right shoulder, its right hind claws in the middle of the back, and its left hind claws in the small of the back. Thus fastened to the back of the ram, with its teeth deeply embedded around the left eye, it had kept a death grip while the ram struggled downward. About the right eye and along the right side of the jaw the skin was full of perforations, showing that the lynx had fastened its claws there while chewing out the eye. Except about the eyes the ram bore no evidence of a tooth mark.

Only the forefeet of the lynx were bloody, but removal of the skin showed a bad bruise on the right haunch, and examination of the skull showed that the squamosal arm of the right zygomatic arch was fractured, evidently as a result of striking against the rocks. The lynx was a male,

135

Lynx capturing Snowshoe Hare

weighing twenty pounds; the ram about twenty months old and weighed 115 pounds.

On reflection I realized that at that time of year an attack on the eyes is practically the only method by which a lynx could kill a sheep. The hair on the neck of the ram was four inches long and so thick that it would suffocate an animal with such small jaws as those of a lynx, should it attempt to bite through at any point other than the throat. As a lynx could not get a throat hold, so the eyes present the only vulnerable spots and they can only be reached from the back.

Sheldon: THE WILDERNESS OF DENALI

NORTHWEST SPECIES

MOUNTAIN LION; COUGAR *Felis concolor* 78 2/3 · 28 3/4 (2,000-730)
A large, powerfully-built, cat-like carnivore with tawny or grayish back and buffy under parts. The long tail is tipped with dark brown or black. Uncommon to rare in forested and broken mountain country, throughout the Northwest, with the exception of northern British Columbia.

LYNX *Lynx canadensis* 36 · 4 2/5 (900-110)
Medium-sized bob-tailed cat, grayish in color (with shades of yellow) with long silky fur that is unspotted on the back and sides. Ear tufts and sideburns are very long. Legs are relatively very long and the feet very large (2-3 inches in diameter). Occurs rarely to uncommonly throughout the Northwest, favoring the dense coniferous forests. Not found west of the Cascades, nor in southern Oregon or southern Idaho.

BOBCAT *Lynx rufus* 34 1/2 · 6 3/4 (875-170)
A short-tailed medium-sized cat very similar to the Lynx but with shorter legs and much smaller feet. The body is heavily spotted and the pelage on the sides and back is reddish to grayish. The ear tassels and sideburns are only moderately developed. Uncommon in forested land, logged areas, and broken rocky places. Numbers have suffered greatly from recent fur trapping activities.

136

SEALS

Like the whales, the seals and sea lions are both strongly restricted to salt water and highly adapted for an aquatic existence. The fore feet are flipper-like, small, used mostly for swimming, and of little value on land. The hind feet are fin-shaped and in many species cannot be turned forward, so must be stretched posteriorly and are of value only in swimming, which is done mainly with the hind feet. The fur is mostly short and dense. Seals are beautifully streamlined and amazingly supple in motion and agile in their watery world. One must look for them in salt water and, unless they are seen on land, only the head and shoulders usually are visible. These are carnivorous mammals and their food is largely made up of fish. Five species occur in the Northwest marine waters.

The Northern Fur Seal bears one of the finer furs in the mammal group and was almost hunted to extinction for its pelt. Now, fortunately, its fur harvest is under strict international control and these animals produce a steady supply for milady's use. Like all such female clothing, however, furs are subject to the whims and vagaries of fashion. The author [Larrison] can well remember a period in the 1930s when every woman, his mother included, could not consider herself properly attired in public without a fur seal

Northern Sea Lion near Sea Lion Caves (J.R.C.)

coat. The price went up accordingly. At present, one seldom sees coats of this fur, but the passage of a few years may completely alter the styles.

The Northern Fur Seal breeds on the Pribilof Islands in the Bering Sea where the young are born, one per litter, to cows grouped into zealously guarded harems by the large bulls. While a cow may weigh as much as 100 pounds, a bull may amount to six times that weight. During the winter migration, Northern Fur Seals pass down the North American and Asiatic coasts, often making a round trip of 6,000 miles. The principal food of these animals is non-commercial fish and squids.

Careful studies of this species have made possible the controlled harvest of pelts. The three-year-old non-breeding males are cropped in part, usually some 65,000 individuals being taken annually for a value of some six million dollars. In the processing of the fur, the coarse guard hairs are removed, to expose the dense, soft underfur which gives the pelts their value. Much credit for research on this valuable mammal should go to a prominent Pacific Northwest mammalogist, Victor B. Scheffer, a leading authority on marine mammals of the world. Anyone interested further in the Northern Fur Seal should consult the writings of Dr. Scheffer and his associates.

Fur Seals (J.W.T.)

137

California Sea Lion

Harbor Seals near Yaquina Head, Newport, Oregon (J.R.C.)

The Northern, or Steller's, Sea Lion lacks a coat of underfur, having only the coarse guard hairs, and thus does not figure importantly in the fur trade. It does, however, get into man's economy through its habit of preying on halibut and other fish in nets and on lines. This species bred at one time along the Pacific Coast on suitable rocky places, but their pupping grounds are now considerably reduced. Sea lions breed in colonies, usually 1-16 cows per bull. The single pup is born in May or early June. Food consists of various kinds of fish, especially herring, as well as squids. This species has been consistently persecuted by fishermen who regard it as a competitor for their catch. Since the number of sea lions have decreased markedly in recent years, it would appear that strict management and protection should be afforded these animals, based on proper scientific study.

The alternate common name commemorates Georg Wilhelm Steller, naturalist on Vitus Bering's expedition to Alaska in 1740-42. While at the place, Steller studied the birds and mammals, particularly the Northern Sea Lion and the Steller's Sea Cow, the latter unhappily now extinct. The Steller's Jay was named after this pioneer North Pacific naturalist.

The California Sea Lion is about half the size of the Northern Sea Lion and varies in color from yellowish brown to black, usually appearing black when wet. It is the trained seal of marine land, circus, and zoo shows, and is a playful, friendly animal capable of being trained to perform numerous tricks. Unlike the previously described species, the California Sea Lion does not breed in closely maintained harems. A single young is born to the female in early summer. Most bulls do not breed until at least five years old; cows, their third year. Food consists of squids and fish. This species has a honking bark, unlike the roar of the Northern Sea Lion. Numbers have been killed by fishermen who consider it a predator on food fish. Investigation has not revealed these seals to be more than an occasional nuisance to this respect, however.

The hot rays of the late afternoon sun blazed down on the motionless waters among the mud flats along the delta of the Stillaguamish River where it empties into Puget Sound. The three kayaks and their occupants moved slowly through the heat-stricken maze toward the end of a trip from the mountains, the purpose of which was to gain first-hand information for a chapter on water for a book on Mount Pilchuck. The mouth of the river had been reorganized since our map had been published and we had come to the Sound several miles below our proposed final destination and the location of the waiting cars to take us back to Seattle. As a result, we had a long paddle to make northward through the pungent flats against an ebbing tide. Suntans were rapidly turning to sunburns. The author [Larrison], having resigned his pants and shirt to a bikini-clad partner of his canoe, was sizzling to a well-done turn in a pair of swim trunks. It was in this situation that we became friends with a group of Harbor Seals. Apparently curious, they pushed their heads up above the water around us, looking us over briefly, and then submerging to change their position. Seemingly friendly and not fearing us at all, they accompanied the party practically the entire distance of our mudflat journey. As this episode demonstrated, this seal is an inshore species, being common in harbors, bays, and other protected waters and is probably the one member of the order most commonly seen by Northwest coastal people.

The Harbor Seal feeds entirely on fish, cephalopod mollusks, and crustaceans, especially crabs. Mating takes place in midsummer with

139

Harbor Seal

usually a delayed implantation of the blastocyst with the gestation of some nine months then resulting in the birth of a single pup the following early summer. The young seal begins to catch fish within a few days after birth and is weaned after about two months.

The giant of all seals, the Northern Elephant Seal, occasionally strays north from its main haunts along the Mexican and Californian coasts to appear in more northern waters. The bull is immense, reaching a length of just under 20 feet and a weight of two and a half to as much as four tons. The female is somewhat smaller. The Elephant Seal gets its name from the trunk-like proboscis which occurs on the snout of the male. When the male is snorting, as in territorial disputes, the proboscis is enlarged and bent down into the mouth where it apparently acts as a resonating organ. Small harems are maintained by the mature bulls. A single pup is born to the female, which was bred during the winter breeding season. The food consists of fish, small sharks, and squids. Although not common in coastal waters, the animal with its immense size and general light coloration should be easily identifiable.

Larrison: MAMMALS OF THE NORTHWEST

NORTHWEST SPECIES

NORTHERN FUR SEAL *Callorhinus ursinus* males: 7-8 feet (2,142-2,448); females: 5 feet (1,530)
Medium-sized dark brown seals with grayish shoulders and foreneck. Females are slightly paler and smaller. The male has a prominent crest on the forehead. Common in migration off the Pacific Northwest coast in late fall and spring and sometimes in winter. Mostly well off shore.

NORTHERN SEA LION *Eumetopias jubatus* males: 10-12 feet (3,060-3,672); females: 8-9 feet (2,448-2,754)
Varying in color from tawny to dark brown, these large seals may weigh a half to a full ton (males). The bull does not have a crest on the head. Coastal waters along the Pacific Northwest, breeding in our region mostly along the Oregon coast. Present the year-around.

CALIFORNIA SEA LION *Zalophus californianus* males: 7-8 feet (2,142-2,448); females: 5-6 feet (1,530-1,836)
Brownish to dull blackish. The male with a high crest on the head. Sporadic visitor along the Oregon and Washington coasts and that of southern British Columbia.

HARBOR SEAL *Phoca vitulina* 4-6 feet (1,224-1,836)
A small grayish or yellowish seal thickly spotted with brownish or blackish spots and blotches. Head is dog-like in shape. Hind flippers always extended backwards. Fairly common in inshore salt waters in the Pacific Northwest.

NORTHERN ELEPHANT SEAL *Mirounga angustirostris* males: 14-16 feet (4,284-4,896); females: 7-14 feet (2,142-4,284)
An immense dark grayish or tannish seal, the male being characterized by a large inflatable proboscis. Uncommon off the ocean coast, mostly in spring and early fall.

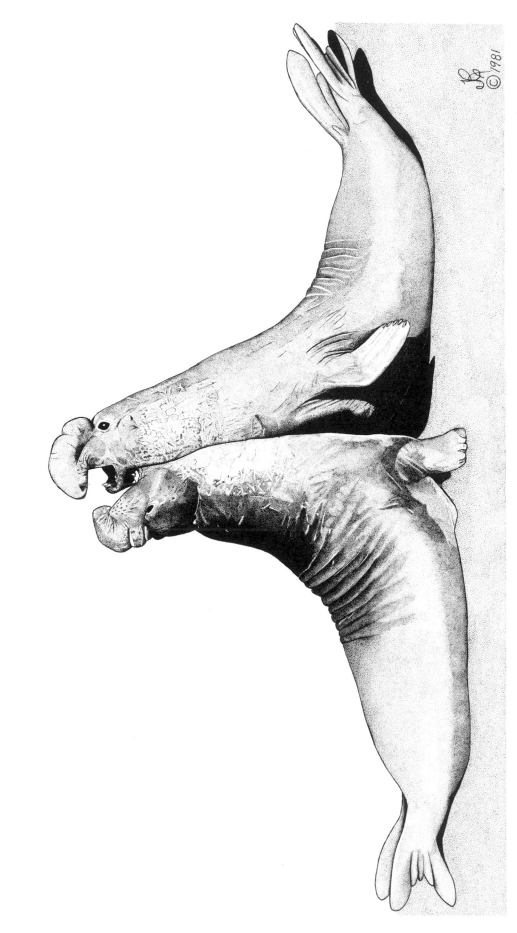

Northern Elephant Seal

DEER

White-tailed Deer in argument (Dr. D.A. Christensen, Kendrick, Idaho)

These fine game mammals [Black-tailed Deer] distinguished for their size, beauty, and grace of movement, are of surpassing value as an asset of Mount Rainier National Park. Unfortunately, they are not particularly abundant, for reasons which are not far to seek. J.B. Flett writes (in letter) that on the south side of the mountain, where there are many automobiles on the road and people coming and going continuously, the deer become quite tame and constitute a very real attraction to the tourists. These tame animals wander over the park boundary or are forced over by bad weather, and during the hunting season fall an easy prey to gunners. In 1918, according to Flett, at least 16 were shot near the south boundary. Cantwell reports that 4 were killed near Bear Prairie, 3 miles south of Longmire, during the first week of the hunting season (fall of 1919). Apparently the only way to affect a substantial increase in the number of deer is to establish a game preserve outside the park of sufficient area to safeguard the deer's fall and winter range....

According to local observers, the deer population is subject to fluctuation in numbers from year to year. Burgon Mesler, of Ashford, Wash., says deer were very scarce in 1900, but gradually increased up to 1916, when they underwent a marked decrease, perhaps due principally to the hard winter.

During the summer months the deer seek the higher levels of the park, where open spaces afford more sunlight and grass. They are especially fond of burns, where the thick vegetation provides an abundance of browse.

During the day deer usually lie under cover of thick brush or trees; but in the morning and evening twilight, as well as on moonlight nights, they roam in search of pasture.

143

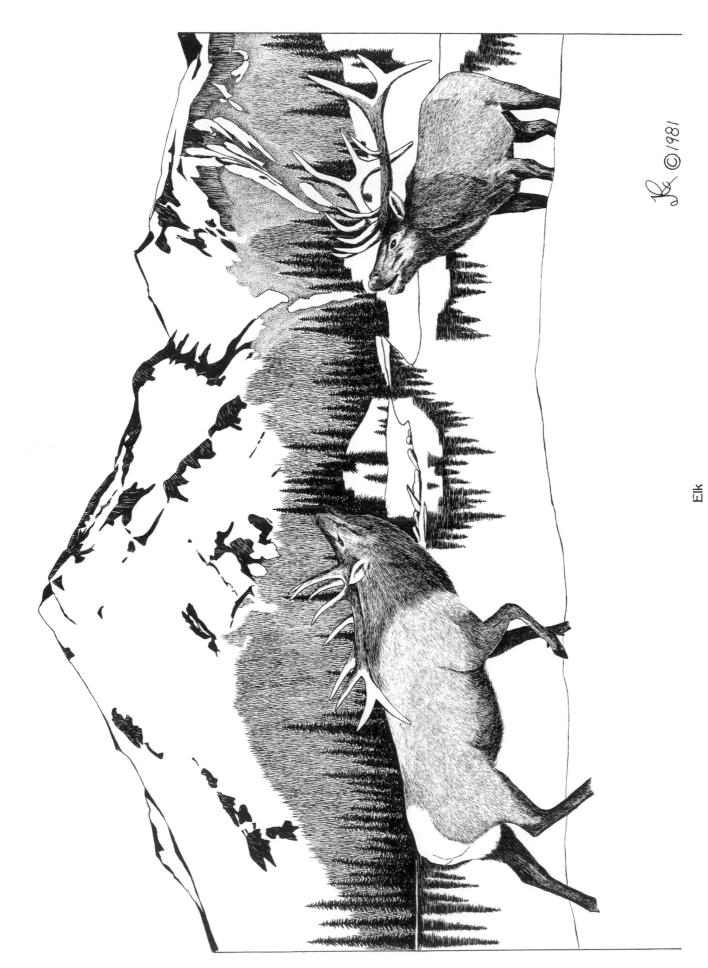

Elk

©1981

There are few prettier pictures than that of a deer on a mountain meadow just at sunrise. The lupines and paintbrushes glisten and sparkle as the light catches their brilliant petals, and the horns of the animal with its alert and attractive appearance impels one to an even greater appreciation of the beauty of the scene. Or perhaps a deer is jumped from among the logs and vegetation of an old burn. The flight of the agile animal is fascinating, as it bounds lightly over the tangle of fallen trunks, comes down stiff legged each time, and immediately leaps again as if each hoof tip contained a hidden spring. For a few rods it proceeds without stopping; then its curiosity compels it to swing about and investigate. It has transformed the blighted landscape of the burn to a region of life, action and interest.

Deer possess a marked sense of curiosity. If one speaks to them or whistles they will nearly always stop and look. They are much more shy in the open than in the shelter of the bushes, even where only slightly protected. In the coverts one can approach them closely, while in the open, 25 feet is as close as one can get.

Fawns are running with their mothers by the middle of July, the tracks of both young and adults being seen thereafter until late in September. The shores of glacial tarns are favorite resorts of deer, as are also the rocky sand bars along the Nisqually, White, and Carbon Rivers. J.B. Flett says that wherever the mother

Elk

Black-tailed (Mule) Deer (Mt. Rainier; J.R.C.)

Mule Deer (Great Sand Dunes National Monument, Colorado; J.R.C.)

White-tailed Deer

ventures into the open the young fawn is con-
cealed in the forest by the doe. If she sees the
observer going into the woods she at once starts
for the fawn and tries to get it out of sight and if
the intruder ventures too close she sometimes
even shows signs of fight.

Deer are frequently to be seen in the evening
twilight near the mineral springs at Longmire.
Sometimes, indeed, they loiter in the vicinity for
hours at a time. Both bucks and does are often
seen also on the road between Longmire and
Paradise. Pete Starbo, road boss, found a fawn in
this region. The little animal was not shy and per-
mitted itself to be petted. Deer are not infrequently
observed in the vicinity of Paradise Inn.

Flett writes that no deer winter as high as
Longmire, though he found a small herd in winter
quarters near Kautz Creek at the west base of
Rampart Ridge. They are preyed on by the bobcat, cougar, timber wolf, and coyote.

Taylor and Shaw: MAMMALS AND BIRDS OF
MOUNT RAINIER NATIONAL PARK

Moose (Mistaya Lake, Jasper National Park, Alberta; J.R.C.)

NORTHWEST SPECIES

ELK *Cervus canadensis* 87 · 4 (2,200-100)
A large deer-like animal, brownish or reddish brown in
color, with a large rump patch. Bulls carry wide-spreading
antlers in late summer and fall. Occurs irregularly in the
Northwest, particularly in semi-open forests and the subalpine areas. Seeks protected "yards" in river bottoms and
canyons in winter.

MULE DEER; BLACK-TAILED DEER *Odocoileus
hemionus* 64 · 5 (1,700-130)
Medium-sized deer, reddish or buffy in summer, and grayish
in winter. The ears are very large (hence one of the common names). Best field marks are the white tail tipped with
black (mule deer variety) or solid black tail (black-tailed
variety). The tines of the antlers are two-branched in pattern,
not with the tines arising in series from the main beams (as
in the White-tailed Deer). West of the Cascades prefers
dense forests and woods; east of that range, to be found
more in open woods, brushy rock areas, large burns, and
open meadows and arid grasslands.

WHITE-TAILED DEER *Odocoileus virginianus* 64-
10 (1,700-225)
Similar in size and color to the Mule Deer, but the tail in this
species is large and bushy and white underneath. When the
animal runs, it is carried as a large conspicuous flag. The
buck's antlers are single right and left beams with the tines
arising in series therefrom. In dense wooded and marsh
areas east of the Cascades, except on certain islands and
river bank areas in the lower Columbia River.

MOOSE *Alces alces* 120 · 3 (3,000-75)
A very large deer, blackish or dark brownish in color with (in
males) large spreading palmate antlers. Stands 7 feet or
more tall at the shoulders. Prefers brushy wooded and
forested land, particularly near water (especially lakes and
ponds) in northern Idaho, northeastern Washington, and
British Columbia (excepting the southwest coastal area and
Vancouver Island). Cannot be confused with any other deer.

CARIBOU *Rangifer tarandus* 96 · 8 (2,400-200)
A medium-sized to large deer with semi-palmate antlers (in
both sexes, though those of the female are smaller).
Blackish brown in color, becoming blackish on the lower
legs. Neck, belly, and rump are grayish white. The head and
neck become darker in the southern populations. Occurs in
the northern and eastern parts of British Columbia and extreme northeastern Washington and northern Idaho. Prefers
montane and subalpine areas of the mountains within its
range in the Northwest.

Moose

Caribou

Mule Deer in winter (Yellowstone National Park, E.J.L.)

Caribou (J.W.T.)

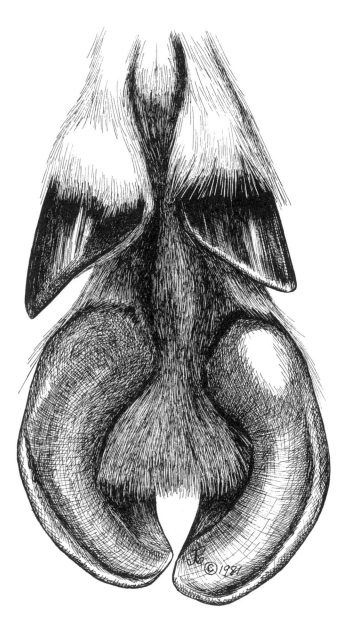

Undersurface of a Caribou foot

PRONGHORNS

Pronghorn buck (Yellowstone National Park; E.J.L.)

In the old days, when one struck a country where little hunting had been done, the once much-talked-of "flagging" of antelopes gave fair sport. By displaying on the top of any rising ground a red handkerchief tied to a stick, so that it should flutter in the breeze, it was easy to decoy a band, particularly during the rutting time, up to short rifle range, for the antelope in its primitive condition exhibits extraordinary curiosity. The shooting itself on such occasions was, of course, a very tame proceeding, but the animals' amusing tactics were interesting to watch. Now approaching at a trot the fluttering rag that had aroused their insatiable curiosity, then circling to one side, or turning back altogether, but looking over their shoulders, till they stopped and again faced the flag, angry stamping of the fore feet betokening their impatience; then, resuming their progress towards the flag at a mincing gait, they would finally, if the wind did not betray the hidden watcher, come up quite close.

On plains that are dead level antelope shooting was often quite difficult work, for even the best Sharp rifle won't shoot into the next county, and judging distances was not easy, and any slight mistake had more serious consequences than would now-a-days follow the same

error in the case of a .256 Mannlicher, which, of course, is an ideal weapon for this sport.

Much has been written about the fleetness of the antelope, no animal, not even the fleetest greyhound, being able, so it is said, to overtake it. That this is not always true I can state with some positiveness, for I know that occasionally one strikes bands of antelope that can be overtaken on a moderately fast horse. I have done so on several occasions, killing one or two out of the band with my six-shooter. Another circumstance for which it is difficult to offer a reasonable explanation is the obstinacy they evince in continuing their course in a straight line, irrespective of the obvious danger into which it takes them. Many a time, when riding in a file over the steppes of Wyoming or Montana, a string of antelope would be seen in the distance making at right angles for the buffalo trail along which we were riding. If we kept on at an even pace the herd would do the same, sometimes crossing the trail less than 100 yds. in front or at the rear of our small column. In one instance, I distinctly remember, a four-horse wagon followed our party at an interval of not more than 150yds or, at the most, 200yds. A band of antelope, numbering between twenty and thirty head, actually crossed the trail in this gap

Lunch time (Yellowstone National Park; E.J.L.)

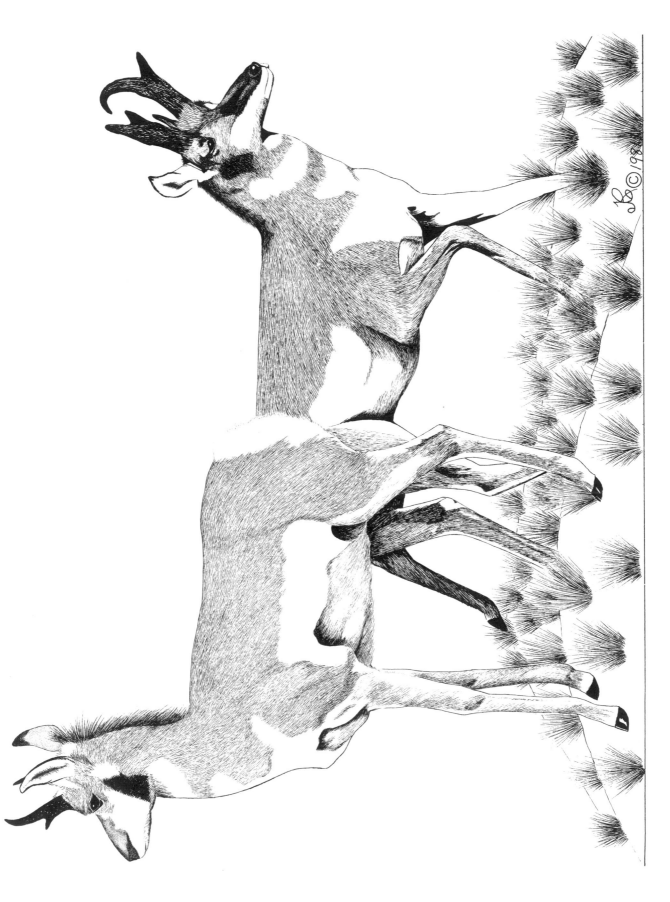

Pronghorns alerted!

without evincing much fear, and as if nothing could turn them from the time they had once decided upon....

The few remarks I proposed to make relate to a circumstance which, until recent years, seems to have escaped the ken of the naturalist, and which even now is the subject of dispute among those who have hunted the prongbuck. I allude to the shedding of its horns, or, more correctly, the dropping of the sheath which covers the core. It was considered to be contrary to all zoological experience that a hollow horned ruminant should shed its horns, that when the first definite information upon this point came before Professor Baird, of the Smithsonian, he refused to publish the letter of Dr. Cranfield of California, in which the latter positively asserted the truth of this fact. Audubon and Bachmann's "Quadrupeds of North America" denies it, for on page 198 we find the following sentence: "It was supposed by the hunters of Fort Union that the pronghorned antelope dropped its horns, but as no person had ever shot or killed one without these ornamental and useful appendages, we managed to prove the contrary to the men at the fort by knocking off the bony part of the horn and showing the hard, spongy membrane beneath, well attached to the skull and perfectly immovable " ...

Ballie-Grohman: SPORT AND LIFE IN
WESTERN AMERICA AND
BRITISH COLUMBIA

Pronghorns in the Tetons (J.R.C.)

NORTHWEST SPECIES

PRONGHORN; ANTELOPE *Antilocapra americana* 58 · 4 (1,350-100)

A medium-sized, horned, hoofed mammal about three feet high with yellowish upper parts and white belly and rump. The front of the neck and chest have several broad alternating yellow and white bars. The short heavy horns project backward at their tips and have a forward-projecting prong. Pronghorns prefer grasslands and open sagebrush in restricted areas in eastcentral and southeastern Oregon, southern Idaho, and the Yakima Firing Range reserve in eastern Washington.

Bison, or Buffalo

BOVIDS

The mountain goat is unquestionably the most interesting animal in the park [Mount Rainier]. Although it is estimated that there are at least 500 of the animals in the area, any mountaineer who obtains the sight of one may consider himself fortunate. Here, contrary to the usual case, the animal is extremely wary; and his Arctic-Alpine surroundings afford innumerable opportunities for eluding observation. Remarkably light on his feet for so heavy-bodied and clumsy-appearing an animal, the goat is able to negotiate ice, snow, and rock slopes of unbelievable steepness. J.B. Flett, who has studied the animals at intervals for more than 25 years, writes that for a long time he followed goat trails through the mountains on the assumption that a man could go wherever a goat could, but he was compelled to abandon this opinion.

The mountain goat's chief feeding grounds in the summer are the green slopes and valleys above timber line. On the approach of danger, he retreats to the higher slopes of the mountain. He likes to sit on his haunches like a dog on the old snow or ice of the glacier, sometimes maintaining one position long enough to melt deep cavities in the snow. In such a place he is doubtless freer from insect pests than elsewhere. When the supply of food is scant at high levels he feeds in meadows below timber line, and when the first severe snows come, usually about the 1st of October, he descends into the timber and brush about the altitude of the terminal moraines of the glaciers or lower, depending on the depth of the snow. He passes the winter in these forested retreats, seldom venturing into the open (J.B. Flett Ms.)

...In traveling, the herd proceeded in a leisurely manner for the most part walking rather than running, and apparently selecting their route with some care. An old billy was always in the lead. In narrow or difficult places they walked single file. In crossing particularly dangerous stretches some seemed to hesitate, but all negotiated the route in safety. As they went they dislodged many stones and much loose slide rock. In fact, their route was

Mountain Goats (Athabaska River, Jasper National Park, Alberta; J.R.C.)

marked by small avalanches with the accompanying dust. On starting a slide of this sort in a rock chute the goat would stop, often on what appeared to be a very dangerous place, and contemplate the bounding stones apparently with interest....

Goat tracks in the soft pumice, droppings, rolling and bedding places between the rocks, and bunches of wool adhering to the vegetation clearly show the presence of the animals even when one does not see them. Bedding places are practically always on eminences such that the goat commands a broad view of the surrounding country while he rests. The animals like to roll or rub themselves in suitable sandy places... If they can rub against a tree, so much the better. One scrubby timberline fir was found with its branches clogged with goat wool.

In the Rocky Mountains, as, for example, in Glacier Park, the goats remain at high altitudes during the winter. Here the snow is swept from the dwarf plant growth and food is always available. Their dense woolly coats furnish protection from the severest cold and storms....On Mount Rainier, however, the precipitation is much greater, and the case is very different. The rocks above timber line are frequently bathed in clouds and storms,

Mountain Goats

and often in consequence are covered with glare ice. Food is then practically unobtainable, and life in the Arctic-Alpine Zone is simply impossible except for such animals as burrow or live under projecting rocks.

Flett relates an incident from his wealth of experience with goats which well illustrates their curiosity where any unusual object is concerned. His party on coming down the north slope of the Puyallup Glacier after a strenuous hike from Indian Henrys suddenly encountered 25 goats feeding as usual on the tender grasses and sedges above timber line. The goats scurried off across the slope and into the upper timber-line meadows. Camp was established about three-fourths of a mile beyond them. After supper and a little rest Flett and a young man named Phillips took kodaks and went in pursuit. The goats first caught sight of Flett, who was approaching them from in front, while Phillips was drawing in on them from the rear. A big billy on a knoll centered all his attention on Flett. As the man crawled in a zigzag course closer and closer the goat became more interested than ever. By this time Flett was only 150 feet from the goat; Phillips, meantime, had approached him from behind to within 30 feet. The billy became uneasy, shaking his head in a threatening manner. Flett tucked his handkerchief under his shirt collar and let it hang down to a point resembling a goat's beard. Then he confidently crept along over the snow toward the goat. The latter began to stamp his feet, shake

Bison (Grand Teton National Park; J.R.C.)

his head, and throw up his hind quarters. Phillips, meantime, had assumed an erect position not far from the goat. Flett attempted to imitate the goat's actions, spatting the snow with his hands and throwing his legs in the air. The goat's curiosity was aroused to the highest pitch. When Flett uttered an imitation *em ba-ah* Phillips laughed. The billy turned and, seeing Phillips standing along side, gave a leap into the air, hitting the earth with a bound at a much reduced altitude toward the glacier, and soon disappeared over the crag....

Taylor and Shaw: MAMMALS AND BIRDS OF MOUNT RAINIER NATIONAL PARK

Dall's Sheep (J.W.T.)

Rocky Mountain Bighorn (Yellowstone National Park; E.J.L.)

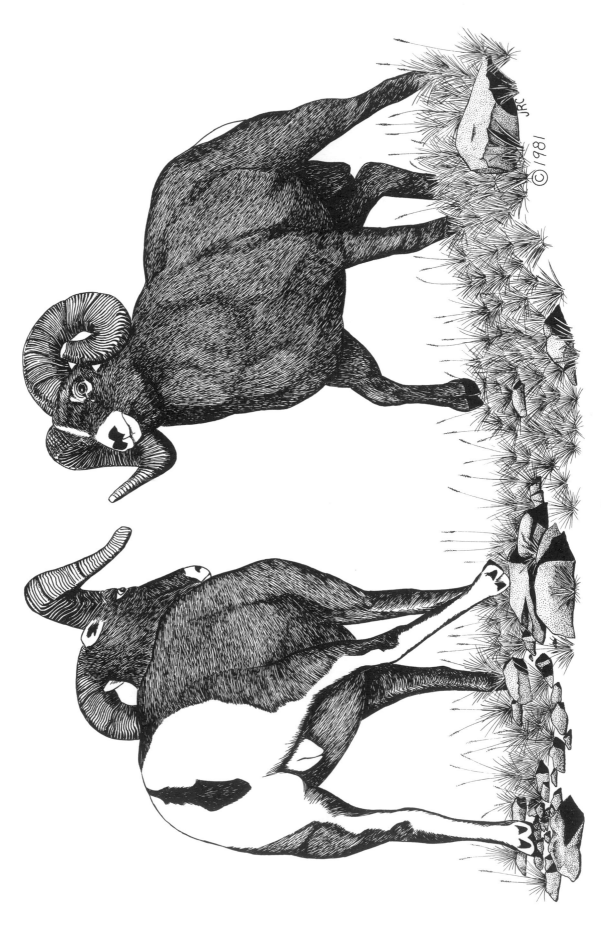

Bighorn Sheep

Stone's Sheep on the Alaska Highway (northern British Columbia; E.J.L.)

NORTHWEST SPECIES

BUFFALO; BISON *Bison bison* bulls: 136 · 24 (3,400-600) cows: 96 · 16 (2,400-400)

A large, massive, cow-like animal that is dark brownish in color with shaggy mane and conspicuous shoulder hump. Horns are short and black and occur in both sexes. Open grassland and scattered woods, mostly in Yellowstone National Park and certain Canadian Rocky Mountain parks; also in the vicinity of these reserves.

MOUNTAIN GOAT *Oreamnos americanus* billies: 64 · 7 (1,600-175); nannies: 10 · 20% smaller

A large goat- or sheep-like mammal with long white hair and black hoofs and short backward-curling horns. Rugged mountainous terrain, especially steep cliffs and high open ridges above timberline in much of the mountain ranges of the Pacific Northwest, including southern and western British Columbia.

BIGHORN SHEEP; ROCKY MOUNTAIN BIGHORN; DESERT BIGHORN; MOUNTAIN SHEEP *Ovis canadensis* rams; 60 · 5 (1,500-120); ewes: somewhat smaller

A large sheep-like animal with short grayish or brownish-gray fur; under parts white. Large massive horns in the male which are thick at the base, then spiral backward, down, and forward near their tips. Horns present on female but are short and curve backward only. Open alpine country in the higher mountains of southern British Columbia, northern Washington, central and southern Idaho, and eastern Oregon. The "Desert Bighorn" variety has been introduced into several places in the Pacific Northwest.

DALL'S SHEEP; THIN-HORN SHEEP *Ovis dalli* rams: 55 5/8 · 3 7/8 (1,420-100); ewes: 53 11/16 · 3 3/4 (1,370-98)

Similar to the Bighorn Sheep but the pelage is pure white in color and the horns thinner and more flaring. The Stone's Sheep variety is grayish brown, except for the white rump, inside of legs, and face. High alpine areas in the mountains of extreme northern British Columbia.

Head of Pronghorn

160

EPILOGUE

We have now come to the end of our pictorial survey of the mammals of the Pacific Northwest. Jim and I hope that you have enjoyed this brief experience with some of the most interesting animals in our region. We hope also that you know a little more about them, where they live, and what they mean to the people of the Pacific Northwest. As mentioned earlier in this book, the population of humans of the region is increasing steadily and living spaces for them must continuously be subtracted from the natural environment. How long will this last? Will the native animals and plants, and the natural environments, be "elbowed" out to make place for *Homo sapiens*? Thinking persons are already concerned about these questions. Just today, a column in the Spokane SPOKESMAN-REVIEW by Rich Landers poses the current dilemma; elk or trees? Proposed timber management practices in northern Idaho — which are the most efficient for taking care of the forests and timber harvesting — may not be the best for increasing the elk population — which the big game hunters desire. This is just one of many problems that will have to be solved in living with our natural resources in the future.

These solutions will require our citizenry to be much more knowledgeable regarding our resources than it has been in the past. Books such as this one, TV programs, lectures, films, special education in the public schools are all necessary to fill this need. One of the messages from Plato's REPUBLIC is that a society can operate efficiently only if its members are well informed so that they may make their necessary decisions in a proper and logical manner.

Will you make an effort to know your Pacific Northwest mammals better, so that you and others may take care of them properly in the future?

E.J.L.

Wolverines

OTHER BOOKS ON MAMMALS

Banfield, A.W.F. 1974 **The Mammals of Canada** University of Toronto Press

Burt, William H. and Richard P. Grossenheider 1976 **A Field Guide to the Mammals** Houghton Mifflin, Boston 3rd ed.

Cowan, Ian McT. and Charles Guiguet 1965 **The Mammals of British Columbia B.C.** Provincial Museum, Victoria, B.C. 3rd ed.

Hall, E. Raymond 1981 **The Mammals of North America** Wiley, New York

Ingles, Lloyd G. 1965 **Mammals of the Pacific States** Stanford University Press

Larrison, Earl J. 1976 **Mammals of the Northwest** Seattle Audubon Society, Seattle

Larrison, Earl J. and Donald R. Johnson 1981 **Mammals of Idaho** University Press of Idaho, Moscow

Maser, Chris, Bruce R. Mate, Jerry F. Franklin, and C.T. Dyrness 1981 **Natural History of Oregon Coast Mammals** Pacific Northwest Forest and Range Experiment Station, Portland, Oregon

Murie, Olaus J. 1974 **A Field Guide to Animal Tracks** Houghton Mifflin, Boston 2nd ed.

National Geographic Society, Washington, D.C.
1979 **Wild Animals of North America**
1981 **Book of Mammals**

Orr, Robert T. 1970 **Mammals of North America** Doubleday, New York

Palmer, Ralph S. 1954 **The Mammal Guide** Doubleday, New York

Walker, Ernest P. 1975 **Mammals of the World** Johns Hopkins University Press, Baltimore 3rd ed

Whitaker, John O., Jr. 1980 **The Audubon Society Field Guide to North American Mammals** Knopf, New York

INDEX